Advance Praise for
The Step-By-Step Guide to Self-Publishing for Profit!

Aaron Shepard, author of *Aiming at Amazon*
"A fine book for self-publishers set to take advantage of today's best entry to self- publishing."

The Midwest Book Review
"Self-publishing doesn't just have to be vanity publishing. *The Step-by-Step Guide to Self-Publishing for Profit!* is a guide [for] making money off one's work when publishing work by yourself. Outlining how to use Amazon's CreateSpace services, [the authors] describe the process intricately and very well. This book should be strongly considered for anyone who wants to get their work out there."

Bonnie Urquhart Gruenberg, Author, *Birth Emergency Skills Training*
"I have owned this book for just a few weeks, and already it is dog-eared and well-worn. The writing is engaging and interesting. Sections include: a comparison of print-on-demand companies, setting up the publishing business, layout and copyediting, promotion and marketing, and interviews with successful self-publishers. I will keep it close at hand for frequent re-reading and reference."

Amanya Jacobs, MA, author, *Getting in HARMONY*
"The authors have written a very useful guide…you'll find clear recommendations and supporting examples. You'll learn pitfalls to avoid— saving yourself much grief. The authors are experienced writers in completely different fields and they offer their expertise to make your process easier. This book guides you from the start-setting up your office and beginning your book- to the marketing of your treasured, finished book. I've already recommended this book to friends who are writing books and I enthusiastically recommend it to you."

Bobbie Graham, Simon Teakettle Ink
"There are many books on self-publishing, but this one stands out because it was created by very specific print-on-demand technology, and the author describes each step in the process. … The book is well-organized and comprehensive … Essential reading for anyone planning a venture into publishing."

Derek Cameron, Author, *A Journey to the Retreat Centers of British Columbia*
"This is a very practical book —precisely the kind of specialized how-to guide the authors say the CreateSpace process works best for... All in all, this is an excellent guide for the publishing beginner who wants to be walked through the process of self-publishing from conception and planning to production and marketing."

Joseph Czarniowski, *Candle in the Darkness Ministries*
"Even if you do not publish with CreateSpace, this book will bring you back to the basics of self-publishing and make going forward an easy step-by-step journey through the jungle of publishing. I am impressed. One of the must-have books for the beginner ... Invaluable to every new author."

Joe Perrone Jr., author, *A Real Man's Guide to Divorce*
"I devoured this book in two sessions, and learned things I never knew before. I have self-published many books, but along the way made numerous mistakes. If I'd had this book ... well ... what can I say? I would be that much farther along ... *The Step-by-Step Guide to Self-Publishing for Profit!* is an absolute must!"

Rebecca A. Emrich, *Living a Life of Writing*
"This is a really great book. [It's] a quick and easy read, and yet, I've learned so much with it. I recommend this book even if you are traditionally publishing."

Jennifer Ochs, NY Book Café, *www.nybookcafe.com*
"This book is a thorough, comprehensive guide packed with knowledge and helpful resources ... the beautiful thing about this wonderful and extremely practical little guidebook is that it allows the author power over their own work. If you truly want to publish your work, there are simple, relatively inexpensive steps you can take to accomplish your dream of publication, and C. Pinheiro does a great job outlining the steps it takes to get there."

Bob Medak, Allbooks Review
"Do you have a book inside you that wants to get out? Have you thought about finding an agent to get your book published? Think about self-publishing instead, especially if you are a new writer. The authors of this book have done the homework for you. All you need to do is write the book and follow the steps to publication."

(The title page should list the title, author, publisher, and the city, like the example below)

The Step-By-Step Guide to Self-Publishing for Profit!

Start a Home-Based Publishing Company and Publish your Nonfiction Book with CreateSpace and Amazon

Author: C. Pinheiro
Contributing Author: Nick Russell
Editor: Cynthia Sherwood

PassKey Publications
Elk Grove, CA

You are smart, talented, and you WILL succeed.
You can make money doing what you love.
Just keep reading.

About this book

This book was formatted in Microsoft Word, and converted to PDF in Adobe Acrobat 9 Pro. The text font is 12-point Garamond. The chapter headings are in Arial. The cover was produced with CreateSpace's free Cover Creator software, with cover photography purchased from Dreamstime stock photography. All copies of this book are produced by CreateSpace using Print-On-Demand technology. This manuscript was professionally edited by Second Set of Eyes.

ISBN-10: 0982266006
ISBN-13: 978-0982266007

Get more free information at:
www.StepByStepSelfPublishing.net

Version 1.5
Fifth Printing, June 2010

Edited by Cynthia Sherwood, *www.secondsetofeyes.com*.

Other books by Christy Pinheiro

- How to Start a Successful Home-Based Freelance Bookkeeping and Tax Preparation Business

- The Chef's Commandments: Maximize Your Kitchen's Profitability Building and Maintaining a Successful, Profit-Driven Restaurant

- PassKey EA Exam Review

- The Enrolled Agent Tax Consulting Practice Guide

Other books by Nick Russell

- Meandering Down The Highway: A Year On The Road With Fulltime RVers

- Highway History And Back Road Mystery

- The Frugal RVer

- Work Your Way Across The USA

Table of Contents

Introduction 15
Chapter 1: Let's Get Started 17
Chapter 2: Baby Steps for Greenhorns 37
Chapter 3: The Rules for Self-Publishing Success 59
Chapter 4: CreateSpace Book Basics 67
Chapter 5: How to Set Up Your Publishing Label with Bowker 73
Chapter 6: Submitting Your Manuscript 87
Chapter 7: Promoting Your Book on Amazon...109
Chapter 8: Marketing Your Book Online..115
Chapter 9: Promote with Book Reviews 125
Chapter 10: Promoting Your Book on the Internet 135
Chapter 11: Interviews and Book Promotion Techniques.......................155
Index 173
About the Authors 177
Endnotes 178

"I was an artist once. A starving artist! My work was pure, divine inspiration. It was a love affair between me and my work. But let me tell you something... being a starving artist sucks!"

-Nick Russell, *the* **Gypsy Journal**

Introduction

Do you have a great idea for a nonfiction book, but you're unsure how you should proceed? You are an entrepreneur—who just happens to be a writer! Perhaps you have a partial manuscript, or even a complete manuscript, and you have been trying unsuccessfully to market the book to publishers. There **is** a market for your book out there! If you want to learn how to build a good writing business that will pay consistent dividends over the long haul, keep on reading.

The main purpose of this book is to help you cut through all the hype that surrounds the publishing industry and learn how you can make money putting words onto paper. Stop dreaming and start living; get your book published and distributed the easy way, and keep all your royalties for yourself! It is possible if you follow a few easy steps. Don't put your manuscript in the money-grubbing hands of a vanity publisher.

This book is designed for working writers who want to make money publishing their nonfiction books. This is not a get-rich-quick scheme, so if you are hoping to make a fortune overnight, it's probably not going to happen. Most authors can expect to make a decent living within three to five years. For some of us, it happened sooner. You CAN publish your nonfiction book and start your own publishing company—all on a shoestring budget.

In less than a few weeks, you can register your own publishing imprint with the Bowker ISBN Agency. Reap the benefits of passive income that successful publishing provides. No more waiting for query responses. No more begging for scraps at the "royalties table."

Writing is an art. Publishing is a business. This book is about writing useful nonfiction: books that *will sell*. Turning a profit is not a crime. You can write and make a good living doing it, and not sacrifice your creative spirit. Writing for profit means that you can spend more time with your kids, your family, and doing the things you love. Start making real money doing what you love. **That's** writing for profit!

Chapter 1: Let's Get Started

"A vanity publisher is someone who will accept an author's money to produce X number of titles for the author *regardless* of the quality, nature, or marketability of the author's manuscript."

-The Midwest Book Review

Avoiding Vanity Publishers

Are you the artistic type with a burning desire to see your words in print? Do friends describe you as creative and talented, with a flair for the dramatic? Do you have a message to tell the world, a message that you refuse to be allowed to be sullied by filthy lucre? Is sharing your work with the world *more important* to you than making money? Then you are the **perfect target** for a vanity publisher.

Vanity publishers are the vultures of the publishing world. A vanity publisher's main customer isn't the book buyer—it's YOU. Their revenues come from authors who desperately want to publish and believe that the vanity publisher is the fast track to a bestseller. The Internet abounds with tales of fraud perpetrated by vanity publishers.

Some vanity publishers get taken to court. Some of the owners even get jail time for fraud, but it isn't long before another vanity publisher pops up to take their place.

Some vanity publishers will call themselves "subsidy publishers," "share publishers," or "cooperative publishers." There are very few genuine subsidy publishers. Although there are some legitimate subsidy publishers, they cater to a highly specific market. The ones that do exist generally service academic books or poetry. A vanity publisher will edit, proofread, typeset, and publish your book at your expense. Traditional publishers do not charge authors for services once a manuscript has been accepted.

A great resource for authors is **Writer Beware (*www.writerbeware.com*)**, a free website that offers cautionary information about vanity publishers and other writers' scams. Don't publish your book without checking out this website and learning a little bit about the scams that get perpetrated on writers. The more educated you are about the pitfalls in this industry, the easier it will be for you to avoid scams.

Don't confuse vanity publishers with Print-On-Demand publishers—they are not the same thing. Here are the definitions of the different types of publishing companies:

- **Commercial Publisher:** Commercial publishers are often referred to as reputable publishers. A commercial publisher is the Holy Grail for most authors. A commercial publisher, generally working with an author's literary agent, purchases the right to publish a manuscript. Commercial publishers are highly selective and only publish a tiny percentage of the manuscripts they actually receive. They handle all the marketing, editing, cover design, and distribution. There are no costs to the author, and the author rarely gets to decide on the final product that gets delivered to the reader. Examples of large commercial publishers include Penguin Books, Random House, and HarperCollins.

- **Vanity Publisher**: A vanity publisher prints and binds a book at the author's sole expense. Vanity publishers may exclude objectionable content such as pornography, but otherwise they do not screen for quality—they publish anyone who can pay, often for thousands upon thousands of dollars. [a]

- **Self-publishing with Print-On-Demand:** Self-publishing is similar to vanity publishing in that self-published authors bear the costs of self-publishing their own book. However, the use of an online Print-On-Demand publisher has made these costs minor compared to the cost of vanity publishing.

By using the services of one Print-On-Demand publisher, **CreateSpace,** an author can typically self-publish a well-designed and edited book for between $200 and $1,000—basically the cost of an ISBN and a freelance copy editor. **CreateSpace** is a Print-On-Demand publisher, printer, and online marketplace all in one! The completed manuscripts and copyrights are owned by the author, who keeps all proceeds from sales. With CreateSpace, royalties are directly deposited into the author's bank account a month after the sale of the books.

Unlike traditional publishers, vanity publishers target the author as their customer. Vanity publishers earn the bulk of their revenues from the authors, rather than actual sales of books. There are numerous ways that vanity publishers (and sometimes traditional publishers too) take advantage of inexperienced writers. Some abusive practices include:

1. Charging excessive fees, sometimes thousands of dollars, for printing and other items, such as marketing the book. If you are unhappy with these practices, vanity publishers often include ambiguous "defamation clauses" in their contracts that prevent you from publicizing your displeasure.

2. Vanity publishers use little editorial oversight. Vanity presses claim to be selective, but many will accept any manuscript that comes their way, even if the subject matter is marginal. In addition, an ISBN from a vanity publisher is the kiss of death. Bookstores and distributors all know who the vanity presses are, and they will rarely, if ever, have anything to do with them. Bookstores will not stock your book on their shelves if it's from a vanity publisher. This is reason

enough to purchase your own ISBNs and start your own small press. An unknown small publisher is a million times better than a vanity press.

3. Vanity presses often breach their own contracts—repeatedly. They make inflated promises and rarely deliver on them.

Look up the history of **_Atlanta Nights_**. This was a collaborative novel written by professional authors—an intentionally horrible manuscript that was submitted to PublishAmerica. After PublishAmerica accepted the manuscript, the hoax was revealed, and PublishAmerica quickly backpedaled and rejected the submission. But the damage was done—the secret was out. Numerous other "sting" manuscripts have been accepted by PublishAmerica, including one manuscript with the same thirty pages repeated ten times. [b]

Vanity presses often publish a manuscript regardless of content or quality. Some authors knowingly publish with a vanity press, placing more importance on seeing their book in print than on turning a profit. If you aren't interested in actually making any money off of your writing, then by all means, use a vanity press. They aren't called "vanity" presses for nothing!

However, if you take the time to self-publish wisely, you can spend little money up front, and still generate royalties on your nonfiction books and other writing products. Why not self-publish your own book and keep all the royalties for yourself?

Cut out the middleman and deal directly with the retailer (in this case, Amazon). Print-On-Demand (POD) publishing services have made self-publishing much easier than before. POD is a printing technology in which new copies of a book are not printed until an order has been received. When a customer purchases a copy online, the order is immediately sent to the publisher that produces a single copy to fill the demand. As the author and the copyright holder, you then receive a larger percentage of the retail price as a commission. That's it.

This book gives you step-by-step instructions on how to set up your own publishing imprint and publish your nonfiction book. There are almost no up-front costs, and you can keep more of your money. CreateSpace has changed the way people publish and distribute books. If you have a useful, well-written piece of nonfiction, there is a very good chance that you can make money self-publishing. In my case, I no longer keep any inventory. I don't ship any books. I don't deal with any product returns. I just write, proofread, relax, and collect the royalties. You can do it too!

You don't even need to publish a runaway bestseller in order to make a fine living as a writer. In three years, I have created a publishing company that supports my family comfortably. I work almost entirely from home. I make a nice living, and I'm not rotting away behind a courtesy desk or working at a lunch counter (both of which I have done!)

This doesn't mean that you should try to do everything yourself. Everyone needs a good copy editor (unless you have a family member or a close friend with exceptional editing skills), and you may even want to consider professional cover design and layout services. But most of these services can be contracted out for a very reasonable price. CreateSpace recently started offering author's services, including editing and cover design.

CreateSpace's author services are pricey, but they are a "one-stop" shop. Authors can order editing services, media releases, cover design—almost anything that you can think of (although you can save big money if you learn how to do most of this yourself). We will go over book design more extensively later on in the book.

One POD company—Lulu—offers professional cover design starting at about $100. That's extremely inexpensive. You can do it all on a budget. If you have the will and the skills—this book will show you the way!

Finding a Real Niche for Your Book

What is a niche market? Niche marketing is the process of finding profitable market segments and designing custom products for them. Niche marketing is the key to success. Focus your research and energy toward a series of products targeted to a specific market. This way, you can continue to re-use the same research material over and over in different ways.

Nonfiction books are easier to market and self-publish because they are generally niche products. If you have a special skill or knowledge of a particular industry, then you will have a much better chance at turning a profit for your books. Self-publishing is about building a publishing business that will provide long-term profits and secure financial support for you and your family.

Successful self-publishing is NOT about publishing your opus, your memoirs, or your personal journey. Don't say that you've written a self-help book for those overcoming alcoholism when your book is actually a long-winded diary of your own struggles with the disease. You may believe that your own life story is absolutely fascinating—but unless you're famous, your personal journey is going to be difficult to sell.

A study guide for the bar exam is going to sell more readily than your personal memoir about passing the bar. A step-by-step guide for raising children with Down syndrome is going to sell better than your life history with your own Down syndrome child. This doesn't mean that you can't inject your own narratives into the books—quite the contrary: your personal experiences shape your writing. They may even make you an expert in the subject. But your personal experiences shouldn't be the main focus of your book. Make sure that the focal point of your book is the dissemination of information.

> "Niche books do best. This seems to be the mantra of self-publishing. Nonfiction books with a well-defined topic and a nice hook to them can do well, especially if they have a target audience that you can focus on."
> **-David Carnoy**, Executive Editor, **CNET Reviews**

Any useful book has a market if it is well-written and *solves a problem*. Buyers want a nonfiction book that answers a question, helps them do something, or helps them overcome a difficulty. Your job, as a writer, is to provide the answer for your potential readers. Your book is the vehicle.

Creating a niche as a self-published author doesn't mean you should only write about one subject. If you only want to write for fun, then by all means write about anything you like. But if you want to make money as a writer and support yourself and your family with your writing, then it's a lot easier if you focus on a few related subjects. That doesn't mean that you have to be bored. There are plenty of interesting, challenging topics that you can write about that will generate revenue and allow you to make a comfortable living doing something that you truly enjoy.

No author's journey is the same. Some authors market their books exclusively online and rarely do any face-to-face promotion. Others make the bulk of their revenues by soliciting their market directly. You will have to adjust your marketing techniques based on the type of material you produce. For example, if your book is on an obscure subject, you may have better results marketing exclusively online. If your book is on a regional subject like *The History of San Diego*, you'll need to make rounds in the community and hand out copies of your book to local businesses that you think might be interested in carrying it. When you self-publish, book marketing is **_your responsibility._**

Regional books must be marketed locally. If you are a gifted salesperson, this may be perfect for you. If you market your book locally, remember that a discount of 30-50 percent off the cover price is customary. You can purchase the book from CreateSpace at wholesale price and then sell the copies to the businesses directly.

In order to sell to businesses on a wholesale basis, you may need to obtain a seller's permit (also called a re-seller's permit). This allows you to sell your books directly to a retailer without charging sales tax. This is because the retailer will charge the end-consumer sales tax. Selling directly to a retailer is often called "B2B sales" (business-to-business sales). Check with your local county office to see if a seller's permit is required in your area.

Selling in person is more difficult than selling online, but you will earn more money on books that you market directly. If you're a people person, you may even enjoy the experience. If you sell directly, you may be required to collect sales tax on your in-state sales. Check with your taxing authority about the sales tax requirements for your state.

You will read about multiple small publishers in this book, and each one has a different experience. The author of the *Gypsy Journal*, Nick Russell, does a lot of face-to-face marketing at RV rallies, RV trade shows, and at RV parks. He sells books directly to his readers at industry events. He has a huge following and his buyers treat him like he's a friend.

On the other hand, Jan Axelson, the founder of Lakeview Research, is content to market her books exclusively online. Axelson's distributor takes care of all her order fulfillment, foreign rights, and more. That means she's free to spend her time doing research for her next book, rather than selling or managing her inventory.

Dan Poynter, the self-publishing guru, uses a variety of different methods to market his books. Interviews with all of these successful self-published authors are at the end of this book.

Most of my books are about accounting and taxation, a niche market. I do most of my marketing online. I use Google AdWords (more on this later) to advertise. I also send out review copies to accounting professionals and students in order to create buzz. I have tried print ads and direct mail with little success. The most profitable advertising for my titles has been online advertising.

Every author is different. Your marketing approach will depend on your book's subject matter and your tolerance for direct customer contact. Most authors choose to market multiple ways—you will find out what works best for you as time goes on. If you have an idea that's unique and useful, there's probably a market out there for your book.

Keep All Your Rights—and Your Profits!

If you want your book to be published, why not simply send your manuscript to traditional publishers and have *them* pay all the costs of publishing your book?

For starters, it's not that easy. Your manuscript would either be thrown in the trash or sit in a giant pile of what editors call "slush" — unsolicited manuscripts that have almost no chance of ever being published. Finding a literary agent increases the odds in your favor, but it is nearly as tough to find a reputable agent as it is a publisher.

Let's clarify the position of the literary agent. Agents represent authors. They review manuscripts and give unbiased feedback. Agents will analyze the competition and then send your manuscript to publishers. If a publisher is interested in buying your manuscript, your agent will negotiate your rights and try to get you a good deal. Most publishers will not accept manuscripts from unagented authors. The agent's job is to work for you— to place your books in front of editors at the publishing houses. However, it's extremely difficult for new authors to secure a reputable literary agent. Reputable agents do NOT ask for money up-front.

For every John Grisham or Stephen King out there, there are 10,000 authors just as talented whose book will never see the light of day because they can't breach the walls the industry has built around itself.

Consider the steps involved in getting a book published. First you write the book. Then you rewrite it again and again. But when it's finally polished to perfection, you can't simply send off your manuscript for agents to read it. For fiction, you must first "query" agents with a brief description of your novel before they'll even consider reading your manuscript.

Agents only request a tiny percentage of manuscripts from queries, and only choose to represent as clients another small percentage from those manuscripts they actually read.

For nonfiction writers, an established "platform" is critical to attracting an agent's attention. That means you must demonstrate, before anyone has even read your manuscript, that you have a built-in audience of people ready to buy your book. Unless you're a celebrity, or you regularly appear on television or radio, or have a hugely-read blog, or sell out speaking engagements, you don't have the necessary "platform" needed to sell nonfiction in traditional publishing.

But let's say you get lucky, somehow, and you do manage to catch an agent's attention. He or she will float your manuscript in front of various publishing houses. But even at this point, the numbers are against you. Most agented manuscripts are still rejected by traditional publishers. There is simply too much competition, particularly for debut authors, and in this weak economy, publishers are acquiring fewer and fewer books.

But let's go one step further and say your book does get bought by a publisher. Now what? You may or may not get a small check up-front from the publisher, of which your agent will take about 15 percent. You will also get a ton of rewrite instructions, and once those are finished and submitted, you may expect more. Finally, a year or two after your book is first accepted, it will get into print. Then what? Usually nothing!

The publishing house will give it to their sales representatives to present to bookstores, and maybe a few thousand will sell. If you want your book to sell, you must take it upon yourself to contact bookstores and set up book signings, and to contact reviewers and seek out interviews.

Traditional publishers are usually too busy promoting the "big names" to give an unknown author much attention or promotion. By the time all is said and done, if you are lucky, you will probably make about minimum wage when you factor in all of the time you have invested in writing, selling, and promoting the book.

Don't forget, whatever you make, it will be a very small percentage of the cover price, and your agent will get a portion of it. So you do all of the work to research and write your book, you beg someone to look at it, you rewrite it again and again, and then you have to do much of the promotion work yourself. And for all of that, you get a few cents for every copy sold.

The publisher, your agent, and the bookstore make most of the money for your hard work.

That's why I say, "*Forget* agents and publishers—write and publish your own material, market it, and keep all the profits!" [c]

The History of CreateSpace

CreateSpace is a direct subsidiary of Amazon, so publishing with CreateSpace is like publishing with the largest online marketplace in the world. CreateSpace is a relatively new company, and its marketplace design has transformed the publishing industry forever.

In 2006, Amazon purchased CreateSpace. Since then, CreateSpace has grown to become one of the major POD (print-on-demand) powerhouses in the world. When authors publish with CreateSpace, their book automatically becomes available on Amazon. CreateSpace allows authors to publish books, DVDs, and CDs. CreateSpace also allows authors to list their e-books and other media products for on-demand download.

CreateSpace provides inventory-free, physical distribution of books, CDs, and DVDs. The company manufactures physical products when customers order, so you never have to deal with inventory and all the logistical problems it creates. The CreateSpace "book on demand" program is a self-service, do-it-yourself online tool that allows you to upload your ready-for-printing PDF book files and make your paperback book available for sale on Amazon.

Through the CreateSpace service, authors can sell DVDs, CDs, and books for a fraction of the cost of traditional manufacturing, while maintaining total control over their writing. With these services, you can make your books, music, and video available to millions of customers by selling on Amazon. You can even sell the books on your own website with a customized e-store. You can also order finished books inexpensively through your account. CreateSpace has prices as low as $2 per book. There are other on-demand publishers (most notably, **Lulu**), but only CreateSpace has the power of the Amazon Marketplace behind it.

When you publish with CreateSpace, your book will be available almost immediately on Amazon and other retailers nationwide. It's the easiest, most cost-efficient way to get your book to market. No more queries and long waits for responses that may never come!

Since CreateSpace is the most inexpensive route to self-publish a book and get it listed on Amazon immediately, the majority of this book will provide step-by-step instructions on how to set up your publishing company and self-publish using CreateSpace. Once you start making more money, you can purchase other add-ons, such as custom covers, logos, and specialty editing services (I always recommend the use of a copy editor). If you want to save money on cover design, CreateSpace offers the web-based "Cover Creator" software that is free.

As the author and the publisher (the owner of the copyright and the ISBN, the ten digit "International Standard Book Number" that uniquely identifies books), you are entitled to the bulk of the book's profits. When you publish with CreateSpace, the book will immediately be listed on Amazon (within 3-10 days). You set the list price of the book, and you get the bulk of the royalties. You can choose to have CreateSpace assign your ISBN, but I recommend against this. Purchase your own ISBNs so that you become the legal owner of the ISBN. Owning your own ISBNs makes you a publisher, not just an author.

When you finally list your book, your royalties will vary based on the list price and the book's page count. The number of pages affects the production cost. Printing costs are also higher if you want a full-color interior. Here is an example of the breakdown:

Sample Book, 136 page count, B&W interior	Price
List price (on Amazon)	$24.95
Wholesale cost (your price for copies)	$4.22
CreateSpace royalty	$14.20
Author's royalty	**$10.75**

As of December 2009, CreateSpace started offering national distribution to bookstores and other online venues. The CreateSpace *Expanded Distribution Channel* gives your books access to thousands of outlets, including online retailers, independent bookstores, and distributors.

In order to qualify for national distribution, books must be opted into the CreateSpace *ProPlan*. The "ProPlan" is basically a $39 fee that CreateSpace charges members up-front. The ProPlan also entitles you to a much larger discount on the wholesale price of your books, and therefore a larger royalty amount. All of my books are enrolled in the ProPlan.

However, don't sign up for the ProPlan until you actually *approve* your book's proof copy. It's difficult to get a refund if you decide you want to delete the title and start over.

BookSurge

On November 2009, BookSurge and CreateSpace merged. BookSurge was an Amazon subsidiary, just like CreateSpace. They were direct competitors, and now they work together to provide POD services and author's services. Not all the details have been ironed out, but the BookSurge website is directing its traffic to CreateSpace, so the merger is official. BookSurge authors have been transferred over to CreateSpace and now CreateSpace offers the same author's services (such as editing, marketing, and book formatting) that BookSurge used to offer.

Lulu

Lulu (**www.Lulu.com**) is essentially an online printing service. You can print softcover, hardcover, and ring-bound books (good for cookbooks and photo-books). Lulu also produces DVDs, CDs, photo-books, and some other niche products. They provide good customer service and a nice product, but their per-book prices are much higher than CreateSpace. Lulu offers volume discounts.

> With Lulu, you can create your book at NO COST– except for the proofing copies you order. Distribute your book to the world for about $100. And you'll be in the Lulu bookstore on top of it (with a nice little margin for those books sold). One caveat: Lulu has discontinued their chat help which was a tremendous aid. I had to wait several days to hear back from their help desk when I submitted help tickets. This is causing me to consider trying Create Space just for jollies.
>
> –Author **Donald James Parker,** *www.donaldjamesparker.com*

The benefit of publishing with Lulu is that you can print just a few books at a time, and you don't need an ISBN. Consequently, Lulu is great for people who want to print specialty products, such as yearbooks, calendars, or family photo albums.

If you have a product that you want to market exclusively on a local basis such as a preschool CD or a local firefighters' calendar, Lulu might be the perfect choice for you. Lulu is also a good option if you want to produce an item that CreateSpace does not manufacture, such as hardcover books.

The biggest drawback to publishing with Lulu is that generally, you must carry an inventory. That means that you have to pay to print the books, and then pay to ship them out to you. Then you have to pay to ship them to your customers, your distributors (if you have any), and again to Amazon's Advantage program or some other retailer.

I used Lulu my first year and barely broke even. The ancillary costs are just too high. You can try using Lulu's distribution GlobalReach program, which costs about $75.

Lulu's GlobalReach distribution service lists your title in major bibliographic databases and makes your title available to online retailers worldwide such as Amazon.com, Baker & Taylor, and Barnes & Noble. The distribution is through Ingram. I don't know any authors who have had great success under this program.

CreateSpace versus Lulu Press
An Author's Testimonial

In my opinion, your book will be much more profitable if you publish on CreateSpace, although Lulu is also a good Print-On-Demand company (**www.lulu.com**). The first year I was in business, I published exclusively with Lulu. In every case, I owned the ISBNs and moved my books to whatever printing house gave me the best price and royalties.

The chief benefit of CreateSpace is that your books will be listed on Amazon within six weeks (or less!) and anyone who buys a book on Amazon will have your book drop-shipped to them directly from CreateSpace.

As soon as I started publishing exclusively with CreateSpace, my sales TRIPLED. Yes, tripled. And my costs went down, because all of the publishing and book submission is done over the Internet. There's no wasted paper, no postage expenses, and you can design a beautiful cover online with their Cover Creator for free. What could be simpler?

In the end, it really is about the money. Once again, this is a business—YOUR business. If you want to write successfully and make a living doing it, you have to turn a profit and keep your costs down.

Some authors really like Lulu. One colleague of mine, Donald James Parker, currently uses Lulu and has been happy with their services so far, although Lulu charges a higher cost per copy. If you are planning to publish your books for an indefinite period, or if you want to make your books available on Amazon immediately, you should use CreateSpace.

If you want to make money without carrying an inventory and dealing with the hassles of shipping, I recommend that you publish with CreateSpace. But if you want to create a yearbook, local cookbook, or other regional item, you may be happier with Lulu.

Blurb

Blurb (**www.blurb.com**) is another POD printer that specializes in small projects. Blurb features bookmaking software that you can download and use. Blurb has received some good online reviews. The printing cost per book is high, though — much higher than CreateSpace. But, like Lulu, Blurb might be a good choice for someone who only needs a few copies of a project. Blurb specializes in high-quality photography books. If you want to print only fifty copies of a beautiful photo book, you may want to consider Blurb. This is especially true if you want to keep the project private.

Publishing with LightningSource

Nick Russell uses LightningSource as his Print-On-Demand (POD) book printer. He's been pleased with both the quality of his books and their distribution system. Lightning Source is a good option if you are savvy about technology and you know how to format your own books and covers (or you have the money for professional formatting and cover design). LightningSource is NOT a good option if you have difficulty using computers.

LightningSource's quality of POD books is on par with the output of traditional print shops. The books hold up very well after many readings. The extra charge for laminated covers is worth the investment.

LightningSource is not for every publisher, but it works for Nick. It costs about $1 to $2 more per book using the POD method, (rather than buying books in bulk and carrying inventory) but he can order any number of books he needs, even a single copy, and have them delivered anywhere within the country, within about one week in most cases. For a 10 percent rush charge, Lightning Source can expedite the order and you can have it in your hands within two to three days.

Because Nick travels full-time in a motor home, it is worth the extra cost of POD printing because he does not have to order large quantities of books and warehouse them. Nor does he have his money tied up in inventory sitting in a warehouse. If he used a vanity publisher and had to order several thousand copies of a book at a time, pay for storage space, and then pay someone to send him copies on the road as he needed them, it would actually cost him more than with the POD pricing from LightningSource.

LightningSource makes it easy to have books delivered wherever Nick needs them, either to a bookstore that places an order, or to a campground where he is staying. All he has to do is enter an alternate delivery address and select the shipping method he prefers.

Nick doesn't invest a lot of energy in marketing books to bookstores, since they are not a profitable venue for him. Because of LightningSource's affiliation with Ingram Book Company, (a major wholesale book distributor), Ingram shows 100 copies of each title on hand at all times for immediate delivery. As part of this arrangement and to avoid back orders, Lightning Source guarantees books ordered by Ingram will be printed and returned to their shipping dock within eight to twelve hours.

This arrangement allows Nick to have his books available to bookstores, either as standard inventory or to fulfill special orders, without any involvement on his part. LightningSource charges Ingram the wholesale price, deducts the printing cost, and credits the balance to his account. Every quarter Nick gets a check for books ordered by bookstores, and he never has any involvement in the transaction.

Using LightningSource, you can get fast delivery of quality books at a reasonable price. Its affiliation with Ingram gives you national distributorship, and it handles any wholesale orders for smaller bookstores.

The biggest drawback to using LightningSource is the technical expertise that you need in order to use them. LightningSource also charges a set-up fee, which CreateSpace does not.

The benefit of having your own publishing label is that you can choose to publish with Lightning Source **and** CreateSpace if you choose. As the owner of the copyright and the ISBN, (we will discuss all of this later) you can publish your books with any company you want.

The Saga of Bad Beaver Publishing

Some authors prefer to self-publish, even when given the chance to publish with a traditional publisher. Carol Leonard's story is unique because she had a negative experience with a large publisher, and then a positive experience with self-publishing. Her story underscores the fact that publishing with a large publisher is not always beneficial, even though most writers treat it like the Holy Grail.

Lady's Hands, Lion's Heart ~ A Midwife's Saga
By Carol Leonard
ISBN: 978-0-615-19550-6

Why I Chose to Self-Publish
By Carol Leonard, NHCM

I was ***this close*** to publishing with a "vanity" publisher, but by Divine Intervention, I was saved!

I was noodling around on the Internet when I saw a website that said, "Warning: Your book will be registered in the name of the vanity publisher and the ISBN is not transferable. It is not owned by you and is not registered in your name. If you do not own your own ISBN, you will not have the rights to your book." Oh my God! This stopped me dead in my tracks.

I had published previously with a large publishing house ("large" as in Viking/Penguin.) It was an experience I didn't wish to repeat. I ended up feeling that I had lost all editorial control over the content of my first book. Well, actually, I had lost all control. The book was based on two decades worth of work I had done with women's groups. By the time they were done sanitizing and civilizing every experience I had written about, there wasn't a naked woman running around in the woods anywhere in the final version.

And the [first] cover they did was horrific; it had nothing to do with the content. I say "first cover" because they finally changed it to one I designed myself after I had such a hissy-fit that I think they feared for their lives. Plus, the marketing of that book was dreadful. It sat on the bookshelves for six months, and then they pulled it. In the end, I didn't own the rights to my own work that I had done for over twenty years. Not good.

I certainly didn't want that to happen with my current book, my memoir, *Lady's Hands, Lion's Heart: A Midwife's Saga.* This book was my life's story, had all my blood, sweat, and tears in the telling of a saga full of joy and pain as New Hampshire's first contemporary midwife. I had to own my story. So, I returned to that website… and my relationship with self-publishing was born.

The first thing I did was buy the ISBN for my title for $99 for a single number. The man I spoke with about this was Bob Powers, a book coach. He said in order to purchase an ISBN, I had to form a "publishing house" —and what was the name of my publishing house? I wasn't prepared for this question, so I blurted out the name of the farm I was building in Maine.

I said, "Bad Beaver."

He said, "Excuse me, what?"

I said, "Bad Beaver…Bad Beaver Publishing." I told him I was going for name recognition.

There was a very long, pregnant pause. He said, "Alrighty then. Bad Beaver it is."

The next step was editing. I opted for the simplest line copyedit feature, as I was fairly smug in my writing ability and my grammatical prowess. How complicated could this be? I was astounded to receive back about forty "balloons," or editorial suggestions/changes PER PAGE! Holy Obsessive Compulsive! It took me about a month and a half to make all the changes that I agreed with.

The editing process made me deeply appreciative and aware of the "faceless" editor's commitment to having me keep my own voice in the telling of my story. I could choose how I wanted the language to be. In the end, the writing is simply "brilliant" (and all the reviews agree with that too!)

Next came the cover…ahhh that cover! I sent Jonathan Gullery my manuscript and a couple of things I liked, but I had absolutely no idea what he was going to do. As I said before, I had a bad experience with cover design, so I was a little trepidatious. (Is that a real word?) Jonathan was working on my cover while I was slogging through the line edits. When he finally sent it to me, I was speechless. I just stared at it. It wasn't at all like anything I had imagined it would be. Then I started to cry. It was beautiful and powerful and a little mysterious. I absolutely LOVE my cover. Really, I am crazy about it.

This next step is an important one that I almost blew off. I had the option of doing book formatting/text layout through professional layout designers. I thought, "Nah, it's all just text, so why would I need this additional expense?" I could do it myself. But because of my positive experience with Jonathan—and the fact that he highly recommended it—I decided to go for it. I think it is one of the best decisions I made in regards to my book's "professionalism." It is amazing to me how many people who know books have exclaimed that they didn't think it was self-published because of the polished, professional interior.

When my book came back from the printers, I was ecstatic. It was like I had birthed my "baby." HA! Little did I know the hard work was just beginning. I think one of the disadvantages of self-publishing is the marketing and public relations of self-promoting. It's a full-time job. One doesn't have the big media "push" that's available to large publishing companies. Many times I would whine and plague Coach Bob about how exhausted I was trying to get media attention for my book. He was very patient and never once told me to stop being such a wimp.

Early on, before I decided to self-publish, traditional publishers said they didn't want my book because it was only geared toward a "niche" market: to midwives and health professionals interested in childbirth, therefore, the numbers were too small. While this is true, in the self-publishing business, "niche" books do best, especially as I have a targeted audience to appeal to.

An added bonus for me is that lately midwifery has become the new, hip Amazonian profession. Thousands of young women have become Doulas—or childbirth attendants—and are eagerly buying my book as fast as it can POD because it addresses this dream.

This is a whole brand new market I didn't even factor on originally! So, at the expense of jumping-the-gun, I'm getting ready to say to those nay-saying traditional publishers, "Na-na-na-na-na."[d]

Chapter 2: Baby Steps for Greenhorns

"You may write the best fiction ever. Your mysteries may make spines tingle and your romance stories may make hearts quiver. Well, I've got bad news for you. Chances are that nobody is ever going to pay you a nickel for any of that. If you want to write fiction or poetry, **first** make your money publishing nonfiction."

-**Nick Russell,** the Truth About the Publishing Business

Publish Useful Nonfiction

This chapter is designed for someone who needs the most basic information about how to write and self-publish. Everyone has to start somewhere, so this information is for the true beginner.

We'll start with the very first things you should do as a new writer. In order to be successful, you have to learn how to create a product that is both useful and attractive to readers. Nonfiction is different from other material. Nonfiction is easier to market, promote, and produce. Create a product that people need and you will sell it. Do you write about breeding goats? How about raising award-winning pumpkins or how to crochet a gorgeous quilt? We all have hobbies we love. Other people are also bound to enjoy your hobby or your area of expertise.

Write about what you love and **do it well**. You'll make money. End of story.

But beware! Some genres are a gamble: politics, religion, memoirs, romance, and fiction are never a sure thing. Any book that is written to advance a personal agenda is unlikely to sell. Some writers are unable to separate their egos from reality.

For example, Susan was a first-time author that I met online. A diehard vegetarian, she wanted to convert others to a vegetarian lifestyle. She wrote a book about how immoral it is to eat animals. She was shopping for a publisher. Her manuscript already had been rejected a number of times.

I asked Susan who the target audience was for her book. She said, "Well…everyone, especially non-vegetarians." Now, this is her mistake. No book is attractive to *everybody*. She couldn't sell her book to children. It's not a great subject for seniors, either. She probably wouldn't be able to sell it to existing vegetarians—they'd already given up meat. And meat-eaters don't really want to hear about how awful they are and how they should change.

Susan COULD have written a vegetarian cookbook, a history of the vegan movement, or a travel book about the best vegan restaurants in the state. These alternatives would have been *useful*. She could have made her point about the vegetarian lifestyle, and still have a useful nonfiction book about a topic that she feels very strongly about. Instead, she put all of her energies into a manuscript that had little marketing potential. Susan couldn't communicate her message, and she wouldn't make any money either.

Nobody buys a book in order to get beat up. In publishing circles, this is called a "bad news" book. The New York Times recently covered this phenomenon with Sylvia Ann Hewlett's book, *Creating a Life: Professional Women and the Quest for Children*. The book was about professional women who delay childbirth in order to be successful in the workplace. Hewlett's book generated enormous publicity. The book was well-researched, edited, and written. It was mentioned on *Oprah*, *60 Minutes*, and the *Today Show*. But it wasn't selling! The reason? The book is depressing. According to the Times, "Women are just not interested in shelling out $22 for a load of depressing news about their biological clocks."ᵉ Don't make your book a "bad news" book.

You are an inventor. Your book is your invention. Useful products sell well. Poorly designed products don't sell at all.

Is **your** book useful and well-designed?

The Problem with Fiction

Writing fiction is another matter entirely. Fiction is a LOT more difficult to market, distribute, and sell. Fiction writers usually use a literary agent and a traditional publisher. If you are a novelist, you don't have to give it up, but you also have to feed your family. People don't "need" to buy a fiction book. Customers can justify purchasing nonfiction (I really need this book because I need to find out how to _____). Here are some other themes that are overdone and fall into that "needless luxury" trap:

- Personal biographies (unless you're famous)
- Your **opinion** about how you "found God"
- Any book with a financial get-rich-quick scheme (buying real estate, etc)—the market is glutted with these books
- Personal journeys of self-fulfillment, soul journeys, psychic missions, etc. (This does not include books that are specifically targeted at Wiccans or scholarly books about the occult. Those actually do quite well)
- Most disease books (a natural cure for cancer, vitamins can change your life, etc.), unless the subject is highly specific and unique

Publishing useful nonfiction is a good way to earn money doing something that you enjoy. You can continue to write fiction if it makes you happy, but writing nonfiction can be your day job.

Nonfiction writers have a million ways to market their books. Trade shows, industry events, speaking engagements (these are called "back of the room sales"), and dozens of other opportunities are available for nonfiction writers to promote their books. You just have to find your target market—and shoot for it!

Your Target Audience

Who is your target audience? This may be the most important question that you ask yourself. Nonfiction writers do not write for everyone. They write for a specific *someone*. You must have that audience in mind when you write and market your book.

In order to identify your target audience, you have to understand who is most likely to purchase your book. For Nick Russell, author of the *Gypsy Journal*, his target audience is full-time RVers. He markets his books and newspaper exclusively to them, with great success. What do you write about? Who is the most likely person to purchase your book? You need to discover who that person is if you are going to be successful.

That doesn't mean that you won't have a secondary audience for your book. Most authors do have a secondary audience—this is a buyer who purchases your book as a gift for someone else, or who picks up your book on pig farming because their father was a pig farmer and they are waxing nostalgic. A book's secondary audience is difficult to target and even more difficult to identify, but always keep your mind open to the possibility that you might have an untapped market out there that you didn't recognize before.

If you write on subject matter for a very narrow audience, consider ways to expand it. There might not be a huge audience for a book about the best Mexican restaurants in your hometown, but how about a book on the best Mexican restaurants in Northern California? There might not be a huge audience for a book on how to brew tea, but how about a book on how to raise, harvest, and brew your own homemade teas? You don't have to be an expert at the beginning. Nobody is *born* an expert on anything—you learn as you go along. Do the research. Make yourself an expert. That's what everybody else does.

There are many ways to determine who your target audience is going to be. The best way is always to examine your competitors first. If possible, get copies of your competitors' books from your local library, or purchase them on Amazon.

Look up all your top competition. Search for your book's subject matter, find the top authors, and look at their books. Amazon has a great feature called "Look Inside" where you can peek inside a book and read a portion. Usually, you can read the table of contents, the introduction, a snippet of the first chapter, and the back cover copy. Soak up all of this information. It's important to your own success.

Even if you don't have the money to purchase your competitors' books, at least take the time to read as much as you can about the books themselves. Look at the subjects the author covers. It will help you determine your own audience, and you might discover things that you missed that will help your own book be more successful. After you are done reading all the "Look Inside" previews, look up the authors online. Every author has a website these days, and many have blogs too. Look them up. Read their websites and their blogs. See what type of people are leaving comments and the type of readers their book attracts. The authors may post certain events that they attend or things that they enjoy. This will give you an insight into how you can promote your own book.

When you finally develop your own website and blog, try to get as much feedback as you can. Listen to the negative feedback too. It's all helpful and everything can be a learning experience to make your book more successful.

After that, you just need to sit down and write.

Set Realistic Daily Goals

Writer's block is for lazy writers, or else writers with colossal egos. If you want to make a real living as a writer, you can't afford the luxury of writer's block. Successful writers do better than hobbyists because they treat their writing like a profession. Start a manuscript. Set a realistic daily goal for yourself. Just do it— it's as easy as it sounds, and it beats washing dishes any day!

Here are good strategies for meeting your daily writing goal. You can dedicate a certain amount of time per day to your writing business. Treat it just like a regular job. Devote, for example, one hour to your website and your blog, and one hour for financial tasks such as bookkeeping and checking your sales. The remainder of your time should be spent on writing or outright promotion. You may enjoy promoting your books on forums, but be careful! Forums often become a black hole for writers—you can spend the whole day posting and very little time writing.

You can choose to set a goal as writing a "number of pages." This seems to be the most popular method for writers to use, and five pages seems to be the average daily goal. Some writers will do less, and some will do more, depending on their background, experience, or field of expertise.

If you decide to use the "number of pages" method, you will eventually generate an average, steady number of pages in any given week. If you approach your writing this way, you will be more successful because you force yourself to produce content that you need to support yourself financially.

My personal goal is always five pages per day. I know that if I can write approximately five pages per day, in a month I'll have about 100 pages of material. Maybe I won't be able to use all of it, but a daily goal helps to keep me focused.

Don't be afraid to abandon a project that you don't like, but try to stick with a project once you get close to the end. You will never make a living as a writer if all you produce is incomplete manuscripts.

It may help you to develop certain rituals in connection with your writing. Many writers admit that they follow daily routines and that this helps them concentrate on the task at hand. Author Lynn Viehl admits on her blog that she is unable to write barefoot, and therefore puts on slippers or socks before she begins writing.

Some writers put on a comfortable sweater or a favorite t-shirt before they begin. Many writers enjoy solitude when they write. Turn off the phone, the TV, and the radio. You'll probably produce better material when it's quiet and you aren't interrupted. Quit checking your e-mail twenty times a day.

Unplug your Internet access if it helps. If you can't write, do research instead. Pick up a book on your subject (preferably a competitor's offering) and start reading. Use all of your valuable time to promote, write, or research your project.

Ten Baby Steps

Let's go over the first ten baby steps that you must complete. You don't have to do all of these in order, but all must be done before you publish your book.

1. A pen name can increase sales and guard privacy

A person's name can be a touchy subject. The choice of whether to choose a pen name is up to you. Actors, musicians, and performers often employ the use of a pseudonym. In the entertainment industry, the use of a stage name is a given. But some writers are uncomfortable using a pen name for a variety of reasons.

There are some prickly realities that we face in this business, and they apply to authors just the way they apply to other professions. Using a pen name is a business decision. Famous authors will often write under multiple pen names, depending on the type of material they publish. Anne Rice, the famous author of *The Vampire Chronicles*, published under various pen names throughout her career. Rice was born Howard Allen O'Brien (yes, her parents really did name her Howard). She published under the names Anne Rice, Anne Rampling, and A.N. Roquelaure. Each pen name was used for a different genre.

Now I know that there are some writers out there who can sell a million copies no matter what their names are. But the reality is most authors choose a pen name in order to sound more appealing to buyers. Unless your target audience is a specific ethnic group, (such as a Vietnamese cookbook, for example) the less "ethnic" your pen name, the better your chance at sales. If your name is especially long, you may want to shorten it. Some genres are sex-specific. Authors who publish romance novels must generally do so under a female name.

Many authors also choose to write under a name that's androgynous, like "Terry" or "Reese." This makes it more appealing to both sexes. I publish under a derivative of my legal name. If you are female, your book may do better if you choose to use only your first initial on the cover. This is particularly true for female writers of technical nonfiction. As I mentioned before, it's purely a business decision, and if you're uncomfortable using a pen name for some reason, then don't do it. But please recognize that it may have a negative impact on your sales.

If you really want to use your given name as your pen name, then do it. But in my experience, the less innocuous a writer's pen name, the better the sales (ever notice how many writers use the last name "Brown" or "Smith"?) And if your book does really well, you can retain some privacy with your real name because all of your books are published under your pen name. If your book does poorly, you can switch to another pen name and have a fresh start.

Personally, I don't care if a buyer has a problem with my race or sex. And you shouldn't care either. It's just business. I want readers to buy my books and enjoy them. After all, this is about doing what you love and making money at it, right?

Publishing Under a Pen Name—Pros and Cons

Fledgling authors should consider publishing under an alternative identity. Here are some pros and cons to consider before deciding to publish under a pen name.

PRO: A well-chosen pen name can improve an author's overall marketability. Many potential buyers choose books with their eyes, and one of the first things they notice is the author's name. If that name doesn't seem to mesh well with the book's genre, they may pass it by. A romance novel written by "Anne Bordeaux" or a sports trivia book written by "Tug McCluskey" would be more marketable than the same works published by "Les Smithson" or "Milton Hackney."

CON: A poorly-chosen pen name could come across to readers as gimmicky or contrived. An author's name should provide at least some measure of credibility or legitimacy. Marketing a book on military history under the pen name "Dirk Ramrod" or a cookbook under the pen name "Mary Rollingpin" would quickly undermine that credibility. Unless the book is clearly in the humor genre, a whimsical or nonsensical pen name should be avoided at all costs. The joke will eventually wear thin.

PRO: A pen name creates anonymity for the author. In a world where an author's personal information can be obtained with only a few keystrokes and Internet access, it makes sense to publish under a pen name for the sake of public anonymity. For unestablished or beginning authors, this practice may feel deceptive or misleading, but many professional writers need to establish boundaries when it comes to personal privacy. Using a pen name helps to create those boundaries.

CON: The flip side of this is that your family, friends, and acquaintances may not find your book. A pen name may be confusing to a writer's established readership, relatives, and friends. Releasing a book under a pseudonym may ensure some privacy, but it can make it difficult for your friends to connect the book with the real author. Marketing a self-published book under an assumed name could also be difficult if the author's real identity already has a strong recognition factor.

PRO: A pen name could prevent confusion in the marketplace. Sometimes an author has little choice but to assume a pen name, primarily because the author's real name is already "owned" by an established writer. Having two writers using the name "Stephen King," for example, would definitely create confusion in the marketplace. Why would a famous horror writer publish a book on home gardening? The author on gardening may have to consider a pen name such as "Steve J. King" in order to avoid confusion with another writer's work. If your name is similar to another famous author's, you should seriously consider a pen name or a derivation so that your buyers don't get confused.

CON: A contrived pen name could become an embarrassment for the author in the future. Sooner or later, the real identity of a pseudonymous author will be revealed. Some writers take on assignments under an assumed name early in their careers for purely economic reasons. If these early works become public knowledge later, it could hurt the real author's credibility with readers. Writing in genres such as erotic fiction under a pseudonym may pay the bills, but may prove to be damaging to a writer's reputation later in his or her career.

PRO: A pen name allows authors to publish outside of their established genres. An established mystery writer may decide to publish a cookbook, or a humor writer may want to release a serious biography on John F. Kennedy. By using a pen name, an author can still publish works under his or her real identity without causing confusion among his or her established readership. This can be especially helpful when publishing a book in a genre where gender or other characteristics are known marketing considerations.

CON: Using a pen name in order to deceive readers or exaggerate credentials can damage the author's credibility and future sales. A pen name should not make false claims, such as the use of fraudulent titles or bogus educational degrees. A book on home or folk remedies does not have to be written by "Dr. Michael Samuels" or "Professor Daniel Peterson" in order to be credible. Using a pseudonym for fraudulent or deceptive purposes can only damage a writer's credibility if the deception is discovered and made public.

Ultimately, the use or non-use of a pen name is between an author and his or her publishing team. As a self-published writer, you're free to release your work under any name you believe appropriate for the audience or genre, but you should give the issue careful consideration before committing to an author's name on the finished work.[f] If you decide to use a pseudonym that is not a derivative of your legal name, you may need to file a fictitious business name statement in order to do business under that name. You do not need to legally change your name in order to use a pen name.

2. Choose a name for your publishing label

This is the next step. You will need to choose a **name** for your publishing company in order to purchase your ISBNs, (also called the *International Standard Book Number*). You can see ISBNs on the back of all books that are commercially sold.

ISBN 978-0-8352-5555-4

52495

9 780835 255554

The ISBN is the 13-digit number on the back of every book that identifies it individually to publishers, distributors, and buyers

An ISBN is a unique, numeric commercial book identifier based upon the nine-digit Standard Book Numbering (SBN) code. (We will discuss the steps how to purchase your ISBNs later.) Right now, you must simply choose a name for your publishing company.

If you plan to publish nonfiction books on multiple subjects, choose a name that is attractive but doesn't limit your ability to branch out to other subjects. Make it simple and easy to remember. For example, if you plan to publish books about dog breeding, you can choose a name like *Dog Day Books*, or *Puppy Land Publishing*. This is catchy, easy to remember, and related to your subject matter. But if you plan to branch out to other subjects, you will probably have to get another publishing name, also called an "imprint."

The large publishing houses all use multiple "imprints." One of the largest publishers, Penguin, has dozens of imprints in the United States and overseas. Penguin also has additional imprints for its children's division. Here are some examples of publishers and their "imprints." This list is not exhaustive.

Penguin Group	Random House
Dutton	Ballantine
G.P. Putnam's Sons	Crown
Gotham	Dell
Puffin	Doubleday
Riverhead	Golden Books
Sentinel	Dial
Viking	Random House Children's Books

Getting an additional imprint doesn't take much work—you just have to add the imprint to your existing account after you purchase your ISBNs, and you may have to file an additional fictitious business name statement. But realize that promoting under multiple publishing imprints takes additional time, money, and work. You will have to buy additional websites for your imprints.

It's always easier to promote one company and publish multiple books all under the same umbrella. So choose a name for your publishing business carefully.

Example: Mary Smith wants to start her own publishing company. She needs to choose one of three business names that she likes. The first two choices do not require a fictitious business name statement because the names include her legal name. The third business name would require the filing of a fictitious business name statement.

Business Names Mary has Chosen

1. Smith's Publishing	No statement required
2. Mary Smith's Marvelous Books	No statement required
3. Sunshine Small Press	Fictitious business name statement required

If you want to do business under a fictitious business name, you may have to pay for a fictitious business name statement. This is easily obtained from your local county finance department (usually you can find an online application by searching for "tax collection and licensing" under your county's name.) Since these requirements vary greatly by municipality, you may want to check with your local city or county offices to find out what is required in your area.

It's very easy to obtain your fictitious business name. In some instances, the application is available on the Internet. Sometimes you may submit the application online, or print out the application and submit it with a check. The form is also available at your local registrar's office, or from your county clerk.

Once you file the application for a fictitious business name, you may have to "announce" the name in a local newspaper. This is the case in California, but some states do not require it. If that sounds complicated, don't worry—there are literally dozens of small local newspapers that cater to just this type of classified ad, and you will get fliers in the mail from at least three or four of them.

You do not need to file a fictitious business name statement if you use your own legal name as part of your business name, such as "Paul Brown Publishing." However, you may be required to register your business name anyway in order to open a business bank account. It may be difficult to cash checks without a fictitious business name statement, and most banks require you to have a business license, as well.

If you choose to forgo a fictitious business name statement because of costs, realize that your company may sound less "prestigious" or "professional"—compare *John Smith's Publishing* to *Yellowstone Small Press* (see the difference?).

You will have to renew your business name every five years or so, depending on the county or city government regulations. In Sacramento, California, a fictitious business name costs about $25. In San Diego, the cost for a fictitious business name is $30.

As for your business address, you have a few options. Most self-published authors start their businesses at home.

You can use your home address or get a PO Box. If you rent a PO Box from a UPS store, you will be able to use the term "suite," instead of "PO Box," which will make your address sound more impressive. Here's the difference:

Prevalence Publishing
1234 Main St, Suite 23
Sacramento, CA 95822

Versus:

Prevalence Publishing
PO Box 14
Sacramento, CA 95822

The first address sounds better than the PO Box. But don't feel bad if a PO Box is all you can afford, or if you are forced to use your home address. A lot of self-published authors run their publishing businesses very successfully from a home office. There's no reason why you can't do it, too.

3. Open a business checking account

The easiest way to keep all your income and expenses in order is to open a separate bank account for your business income and expenses. Shop around—there are many banks that offer free checking accounts. Choose a free account or an account with a low monthly fee. All of your CreateSpace revenues should go into your business account. All of your business expenses should come out of your business account and/or a dedicated credit card.

If you work as a part-time freelancer, a separate bank account gives you more protection in the event of an IRS audit. A separate account shows that you are serious about writing—it's not just a hobby.

For example, if you are operating your business through your personal checking account and aren't keeping anything but the most minimal of records, the IRS may determine that many of your expenses are "personal" rather than business expenses.

Although you may be able to successfully defend your purchases as legitimate business expenses in United States Tax Court, do you really want to go that far? Make your bookkeeping tasks easier from the very beginning. Get a separate account for your writing business and make sure you keep your receipts and bank statements.

Get a dedicated credit card just for your business purchases. Don't use it for personal items. You will find yourself being more careful with your purchases when you are tracking them. You should use this separate credit card only for writing expenses, such as office supplies, business travel, continuing education, seminars, and other deductible expenses.

Keeping track of your business expenses isn't hard when you have a dedicated bank account and a dedicated credit card. It takes the guesswork out of bookkeeping and makes it much easier at tax time. You have to keep track of all of your writing expenses in order to write them off on your tax returns. This is just common sense.

Keep your receipts. I use a shoebox (a big one). Yes, I'm an accountant by trade, and I use a shoebox for my own monthly receipts! I reconcile my bank statements once a month using QuickBooks accounting software. QuickBooks is easy to use and is designed for the general public, not just accountants. It only takes me an hour every month to reconcile my bank statements. I staple my receipts to the monthly reconciliation reports. It takes very little time, and I always know what my profit or loss is from month to month.

Quicken is a good program too, and it's easier to learn. Quicken is basically a computerized check register, but you can also use it to print reports and invoices. You can even use an Excel spreadsheet or an old-fashioned journal to keep track of your expenses. Whatever method you use, be consistent. If you have questions about the deductibility of an expense, call your tax adviser, or look it up on the IRS website at ***www.IRS.gov***.

A lot of credit cards offer excellent discounts and airline miles. These are great perks for any business owner who occasionally has to travel. And, if you are a travel writer or go to book shows, you have an instant tax write-off!

Always keep your personal bank account separate. When you want to take money out of your business account for personal use, cut yourself a check and write "owner draw" on the check. This will tell your accountant that you are taking the money out for personal use. As you become a better businessperson, you will learn to be frugal with your personal expenses and more liberal with your business expenses (since you know that they can be written off).

It goes without saying that you should get competent financial advice if you have tax questions. You can usually meet with a tax adviser for about $100-$250.

Some will agree to meet with you for free if it is an initial consultation. If you can't afford a tax adviser, read as much as you can about how to properly file your own tax returns. One of the best books on the market for small businesses is *Taxes for Dummies*. It's an easy read, and designed for the layperson.

The IRS is not to be toyed with. A CPA or an Enrolled Agent[g] can help you file your tax returns and answer your tax questions. A good financial adviser is worth the price. Good financial advice can help you avoid a crippling IRS audit and keep you on track for success.

A good rule of thumb is to keep all records for at least three years **after** the date you file your tax return. If the records pertain to asset purchases (such as a computer or machinery), you should keep the records for as long as you retain the asset.

Employment tax records (payroll and employee records, if you have employees) should be kept for a minimum of four years. Even the IRS admits that during an audit, most business deductions are disallowed because of poor recordkeeping, not because of taxpayer fraud.

Avoid Bad Bookkeeping Mojo

Because I wasn't generating much revenue the first year, I used my PayPal account and also my personal account to pay business expenses. This became a bookkeeping nightmare at tax time! I had paid for many items with cash, my debit card, and also on a few separate credit cards while trying to make ends meet.

Putting all of my income and expenses together at the end of the year took forever. I spent almost forty hours completing a set of books so that I could file an accurate tax return. I swore—never again!

The second year, I started publishing with CreateSpace and opened a dedicated checking account. All of my book revenues went in there via direct deposit so setting up everything was easy. I also signed up for an overdraft line of credit, which covered all the overdrafts when I had to purchase my own inventory or buy supplies and my bank account was cash-poor. I paid for all of my expenses out of my business account, and bookkeeping was a snap! I do all my bookkeeping once a month. Easy!

Business records include things like copies of invoices, cancelled checks, and writing contracts. You should also keep receipts for all of the merchandise and purchases you've made over the year. You should keep the receipts for things like shipping supplies, postage, writing seminars, and inventory purchases. However, this doesn't mean you have to keep paper receipts.

Physical records are no longer required. The IRS allows you to retain scanned copies on your computer rather than paper receipts, if you wish to go paperless.[1] This is especially good news for people who have a lot of "heat transfer" receipts (like the type you get at a gas pump), because these eventually fade and become illegible.

My advice is to make photocopies or scans of heat transfer receipts since they eventually become impossible to read and therefore may be disallowed during an IRS audit.

If you plan to travel to promote your book or do research, keep a detailed log of your mileage. Just keep a little booklet in your car and write down every time you use your car for business. Every trip to the post office, to pick up office supplies, etc. adds up. It's a tax deduction, and with high gas prices, you will get a great tax break if you keep good records.

4. Get professional business cards and stationery

You're in business—let's make it official. A nice business card and letterhead indicates professionalism and shows that you are serious about your writing. When you send out correspondence, professional stationery is like a miniature advertisement for your business.

If you have a good eye, you can use the templates provided by online stationery suppliers, such as ***www.VistaPrint.com***, at very reasonable prices. You don't need to buy very much, especially at the beginning, but you should make a small investment in your new company. You can also purchase fine paper and print your own stationery using your home printer. This is probably the cheapest option and should cost less than $10. It also allows you to print only as much as you need.

Hand out your business cards everywhere you go: in restaurants, at mixers, and to friends. You never know who your next customer will be. People are more likely to keep business cards with a photograph on them. This is why real estate agents commonly use their photographs on business cards.

5. Invest in a separate phone number

A separate telephone number is highly suggested. It can be a cellular phone, landline, or VOIP line. The cheapest way to do this is to buy an inexpensive,

---

[1] IRS Revenue Procedure 97-22

pre-paid cellular phone. For about $20, you can purchase an inexpensive cell phone with Tracfone. Tracfone is the most popular pre-paid cell phone provider in America and for good reason—it's the cheapest and its coverage is good. No bills, no contracts, and no big bill surprises! It's the easiest way to get a separate phone line for your business without spending a fortune or making any long-term commitments. And if you rarely use the phone, it will only cost you about $10 a month to maintain service.

You can use this inexpensive cell phone as your "business line," and post the number on your website. This helps add credibility to your new publishing company, and it shows that you plan to be around for awhile. If you choose to keep specific business hours, you won't have to answer the phone at a time when you are "off duty."

Separate phone numbers may also be available as an add-on to your existing home landline with Distinctive Ring service from your phone company. It is important for your contacts or clients to have a reliable means to contact you. If your kids answer the phone and take messages, you may never get them and that means lost business. Do not let your children answer your business phone number!

There will come a time when you will probably want to get another line, possibly for your fax and/or modem. But to start, use your existing resources as much as possible and keep your expenses down.

6. Join professional organizations

Because making business contacts through networking is so important to new businesses, it's important that you set aside at least $50 to join a professional organization. If you have not already done so, I recommend that you join Writer's Market Online (**www.writersmarket.com**). It costs $39.99 for a one-year, online subscription. When you join, you'll receive marketing tips and valuable business advice. It's an excellent resource for writers, and the information provided by Writer's Market is extremely helpful.

For traditional publishing, Publishers Marketplace is an essential resource and costs $20 a month. This resource may be helpful for self-publishers too. Among other information, Publishers Marketplace shows most of the deals for books in all genres, including nonfiction, so someone would know if a book on the same topic was going to be issued by a traditional publisher.

You'll get information on events, continuing education, and networking opportunities. There are other memberships that add credibility to your business; the organization is essentially lending its credibility to you as a member. Here are some other great organizations to check out:

- **SPAWN: Small Publishers, Artists, and Writers Network (www.spawn.org):** Spawn offers information on writing and publishing. It also offers links to research sources, publishers, printers, and the media. It's recommended by Writer's Digest as one of the best websites for writers.
- **Poets & Writers (www.pw.org):** Offers information, support, and guidance for creative writers. Founded in 1970, it is the nation's largest non-profit literary organization serving poets, fiction writers, and creative nonfiction writers. The national office is located in New York City. The California branch office is located in Los Angeles.
- **Freelance Writing Organization: (www.fwointl.com):** An online resource that includes an extensive database, employment listings, and other reference materials to help writers. This website was voted one of Writer's Digest's Top 101 websites for writers. Best of all, it's still free!
- **Absolute Write (www.absolutewrite.com):** An online magazine for beginning writers and professional writers. The site covers nonfiction, screenwriting, freelance writing, novels, and other genres.

There are also multiple writers' organizations targeted to specific groups or industries. Examples include:

- **The International Women's Writing Guild** (*www.iwwg.com*): An organization just for female writers.
- **The Truck Writers of North America** (*www.twna.org*): A support organization dedicated exclusively to writers for the trucking industry.
- **Christian Writers Fellowship International** (*www.cwfi-online.org*): An organization dedicated to Christian writers.
- **Garden Writers Association** (*www.gardenwriters.org*): GWA is the non-profit association dedicated to professionals in the field of gardening communication.
- **The National Association of Science Writers** (*www.nasw.org*): Formed in 1955, the NASW is the leading organization for freelance and professional science writers.

You should be able to find a professional writing organization related to your industry too. It is always helpful to research and join organizations specific to your industry.

It will add credibility to your portfolio, and you can post your professional memberships on your own website. Join newsgroups, follow blogs, post in forums—and always make sure your signature includes your book title, or your website, like this:

Christy Pinheiro:
www.christypinheiro.com

Every person that reads your blog, review, or forum post will see your name and book title. More free publicity for you!

7. Set a reasonable and regular work schedule

Even though you are essentially your own boss, it is important to set up a reasonable work schedule and stick to it. Your sanity and home life depend on your ability to keep your work and your home life separate. This can be difficult for some home-based entrepreneurs; some find it hard to get motivated, and others don't know when to stop!

You should treat your new home-based writing business as a genuine business with set hours and a schedule. If you are working a full-time job, set aside at least eight to ten hours per week for writing and the promotion of your writing business. Although this will not always be easy, you should set firm boundaries for yourself. At least 20 percent of your time should be dedicated to your book promotion, blogs, and research. The rest of your time should be spent writing.

8. Prepare your home office

Make sure your home office is clean, organized, and free of clutter. Get a pretty plant or a nicely-framed print. If your home office is full of books, clutter, or exercise equipment, it will be harder to concentrate on your writing tasks. Try to avoid distractions. If possible, your office should be isolated from family gathering places, away from the living room or kitchen.

Make sure that your home office is secure. You should also have a shredder in your office to properly dispose of any documents that include confidential information, such as bank statements. Consider investing in an alarm system. Some of the best security companies charge as little as $30 a month. It is an investment in your safety and security, and well worth the money.

9. Always back up data

Always back up your writing data. You won't understand the sheer terror of losing all your hard drive information until it actually happens to you. What would happen if all your projects disappeared? What if your laptop is stolen? Believe me, it's terrifying.

The cheapest way to do this is to purchase an inexpensive backup drive, such as a thumb drive. You can purchase an inexpensive thumb drive for about $20 that will hold most of your Word documents and photos. If you really want to keep costs down, you can just back up to a CD. However, these two methods are not a cost-effective way to back up an entire computer on a regular basis.

I recently signed up for Carbonite,[2] which is an online back-up that sits right on your desktop. If you have Internet access, Carbonite will back up your stuff in the background.

It's all automated. I downloaded the software, which took about 5 minutes, and then it started backing up my hard drive, quietly, in the background. It's not immediate. The first initial back-up can take days, or even weeks if you have a lot of files. My first complete back-up took three days. Carbonite costs about $60 bucks a year, which is very reasonable. I was nervous about losing all my manuscripts to a house fire or computer failure. An off-site back-up made me feel more secure.

10. Start-up costs and potential revenue

If you have a well-written niche product, it will be easy to generate revenue from your book. But it won't happen overnight. Your book will need to be listed on Amazon for at least a few months before you start to see good sales figures. I usually tell people that you should estimate about three to five years in business before you can support yourself entirely from your writing. If you're also working a full-time job, it may take longer.

The first year is the hardest. In my own experience, I worked full-time the first year and wrote whenever I had free time. The second year, I worked part-time and wrote about twenty hours per week. By the third year, I was writing full-time and working only about eight to ten hours a week at an accounting firm just to keep my tax and accounting skills sharp (since most of my income is from financial writing).

Your experience may be different. You may already write for a living, or you may be working in the industry that you wish to write about, and you intend to continue working. Whatever your eventual goals, you can write as much as you wish, but understand that your revenues will always be impacted by how much time you dedicate to your writing business.

---

[2] The authors or publisher are not affiliated with Carbonite, and have received no compensation or consideration for the mention of this product, or any other product, website, or service in this book.

You may already have most of these items, but this spreadsheet should give you a rough estimate of how much you will have to spend on basic items to start your writing career.

Home Office Start-Up Costs (sample)

Goods Purchased	Used/Low-End	New/ High-End
Desk and chair	$35	$550
Computer	$150	$1,500
Printer	$22	$350
Business Cards & Stationery	$10	$150
Software (Word, Excel, etc)	(Student Editions) $199	$1,500
Separate Phone Line and/or Fax	$25	$200
Document Shredder	$15	$100
Backup Device	$15	$150
Professional Organization Dues	$39	$250
Estimated Start-up Costs	**$510**	**$4,750**

These are only theoretical start-up costs for a start-up writer. If you already own a computer, desk, or chair, your costs will be lower. If you decide to purchase a refurbished computer, you will save money on your start-up costs.

Your software will probably be your biggest expense, but you may be able to purchase older copies of the software at a discounted price at online auction sites like eBay. And if you are a student (even part-time) you get discounts on software as well. At the time of this writing, students can purchase Microsoft Office at a 50 percent discount online and at most student bookstores on campus. A great website to purchase student copies of software is *www.AcademicSuperstore.com*.

The software is the same, but there is a hefty student discount, if you can prove enrollment in a college course. A lot of the websites will even allow you to purchase software for your high school children at reduced prices. At the time of this printing, you can purchase Adobe Acrobat Pro for $98 on Academic Superstore's website. This is a whopping **80 percent off** the regular retail price.

"Bare bones" items are what you need to get started. Don't purchase fancy formatting software at the beginning. You won't need it. Let your finances be your guide. Just remember, there's nothing wrong with the pay-as-you-go method, and you don't really need the latest and greatest in hardware.

Buy what you need and the best you can afford, but no more. Remember, your writing is supposed to support you, not the other way around. Think in terms of how long it will take for each new piece of equipment or software to more than pay for itself. Here's a short review list of what is "bare bones" in order to get started:

- Computer with a cable, DSL, or Wi-Fi connection
- Inkjet or laser printer
- Recent version of Microsoft Office and Adobe Acrobat (I still use Microsoft Word 2003)
- E-mail account
- Separate telephone number with voicemail or an answering machine
- Box of CDs and a couple of reams of copy paper
- Business cards and stationery
- A backup device, such as a USB drive

A few of the above items need some brief explanation. Your computer doesn't have to be cutting edge, but don't use a relic either. An Internet connection (NOT dial-up if at all possible) is a must because e-mail has become imperative in this field. You will need to have a reliable Internet connection if you want to self-publish and promote your books online.

A printer is not as vital as it used to be since much of your work will be delivered via direct upload, e-mail, CD, or flash drive. But some writers like to see their work in hard copy also. Don't even think about submitting a handwritten manuscript, anywhere, EVER. Many publishers continue to receive handwritten manuscripts on a regular basis. Unless you're famous, no one is going to slog through your handwritten scribble. Type it up, or forget it.

Now, as for the costs for actually setting up your book, there aren't any. CreateSpace doesn't charge set-up fees. And if you purchase your own set of ISBNs and get yourself your own publishing imprint, then you can publish up to ten books with the ISBNs you have purchased. We'll discuss this in more detail later.

Chapter 3: The Rules for Self-Publishing Success

"Self-publishing can be a wonderful solution for getting into print. It puts you in control of your own destiny and positions you to be a lot more profitable than going with a royalty publisher."

-Marilyn Ross, author of *The Complete Guide to Self-Publishing*

The Top Ten Rules

Becoming a successful self-publisher doesn't happen by accident. To make money in this business, you have to treat it exactly like that – a business. That doesn't mean you have to sacrifice your creativity. You have to be just as dedicated to running your publishing business as you are to your actual writing.

Success doesn't happen overnight, but it *will happen* if you stay dedicated and continue to work hard. You may not get rich, but you'll make real money and you won't be punching a clock! Following these ten rules will help you achieve your goal of success in the self-publishing business.

1. Do your homework

Read everything you can on the publishing business, with an emphasis on self-publishing. Any good bookstore should have a decent selection of books on self-publishing, and you can find even more online. Amazon has an excellent selection, and their prices are great. The more you learn about self-publishing, the better chance you have at success.

Two especially good resources are *The Right Way to Write, Publish, and Sell Your Book* by Patricia Fry, and *The Self-Publishing Manual* by Dan Poynter. Poynter is a writer and a self-made millionaire; his story is the stuff of legend. Poynter's self-publishing book is one of the finest in the industry. He carries his own inventory and manages a great deal of the order fulfillment himself. He also sells to bookstores and other retail outlets.

If you're looking to self-publish your book and do the distribution and order fulfillment yourself, buy Dan Poynter's book. His book is still important, even in the new era of Print-On-Demand publishing because many writers enjoy doing face-to-face marketing. If you like direct selling, there's no reason why you can't promote your book in person. Many self-published writers start out carrying some inventory and doing a lot of point-of-sale marketing themselves.

You can also choose a middle ground. You can fulfill some of your own book orders and sell individual copies on your website, but primarily sell through Amazon. Read the interviews at the end of this book for differing viewpoints about self-publishing. You will eventually discover the right path for you.

There's a steep learning curve at the beginning, but you can avoid most of the major problems that new authors face if you just try to learn as much as you can up-front. There's also a lot of very good information on self-publishing on the Internet. Invest some time in doing online research. But beware! There is a lot of contradictory information out there, so you have to sort the wheat from the chaff.

2. Identify your market and know your competition

Before you type your first line, ask yourself, "Who will want to buy this book?" Identify your market and know what that market is looking for. Then supply it to them. You may think a study of gerbil genetics is absolutely fascinating, but how many other people will? However, there may be enough pet lovers who will buy a book on how to keep their pet gerbil healthy and happy.

You can write the best book in the world, but if you don't have any idea who will want to purchase it and a solid marketing plan to reach those people, all you will do is waste time and money.

Who else has written about the same subject? Study what they have done and figure out how you can do a better job. Will a new slant on the same topic sell? Can you expand on what's already out there by offering more resources to help readers learn and understand more? What can you do that the competition hasn't done?

3. Get a copy editor

Once you have written your book, have it professionally proofread and edited. Get a good copy editor. They're worth every penny. Nothing turns a reader off more than trying to fight their way through typos, bad spelling, and terrible grammar. And don't be offended when your copy editor says something you wrote sounds unclear. If your editor can't understand it, there's a good chance your readers won't either. Let the copy editor do his or her job. No matter how meticulous you are as a writer, your book will go through at least a few rounds of edits before it is ready to be published.

4. Come up with a good descriptive title

Forget artsy titles. These days, in the age of the Internet, "keywords" are king. Make sure your title includes the words that your buyer will be using to SEARCH for your book. Think about every search you ever made on Google—you want the perfect answer to your question, so you try to add all the keywords that might help you find it, right? The same concept applies to your book title. Don't agonize about being wordy. Get your point across with applicable keywords that will help your buyers find YOUR book.

If you wrote a book on how to make money raising earthworms, title your book something simple like *Raising Earthworms At Home for Profit*. A good title will help sell your book, while a bad one can kill it. A subtitle also helps describe and sell nonfiction books. You can expand your book's search profile by using complementary keywords in your subtitle. See the examples below:

Title: Starting Your Own Home Business
Subtitle: A Beginner's Guidebook for Starting a Home-Based Business Venture

Title: The Chef's Commandments: Maximize Your Kitchen's Profitability
Subtitle: Building and Maintaining a Successful, Profit-Driven Restaurant

Title: Advanced Handgun Shooting Techniques
Subtitle: A Tactical Guide for Experienced Marksmen

In all of the above examples, the subtitle helps expand the book's keywords. More keywords help buyers find the book online. Your subtitle can be long and can even include redundant words (synonyms). The easier it is for buyers to find your book, the higher your sales will be.

5. Keep your cover simple and professional

Lay out your book in a professional manner, or have someone with graphics experience lay it out for you. Again, don't go overboard. If you don't have the money for professional layout, don't do anything fancy that will affect your book's marketability. Keep it simple! Colored pages, weird typefaces and other "tricks" will not make up for poor content, but they **will** distract from a good read. Pick a cover typeface that is easy to read. Don't use a cursive or cartoony typeface. It just looks ridiculous.

CreateSpace's Cover Creator software is a free tool that will allow you to produce a very nice cover if you use it correctly. The cover of this book was designed by CreateSpace's Cover Creator, with stock photography from *www.DreamsTime.com*.

Get a nice, subject-appropriate picture for your book cover. If your book is about breeding Chihuahuas, then get a professional photo of a Chihuahua puppy. Don't use an amateur photo. Amateur photos make books look cheap. You can buy professional stock photography online (think $7-$25).There are dozens of great resources for stock photography on the web.

Get opinions about your cover from lots of family or friends and trust their judgment. This isn't about you. This is about getting your book published, sold, and read. Your cover can sell a lot of books if it's done competently. It does not have to be a multi-colored work of art that brings tears to the eyes of strong men, but an attractive cover will pay off.

Above all else, make sure the title is easily legible.

6. Don't neglect the basics!

Understand the components any good book needs, including an ISBN, copyright notice, and other front matter (this is all the publisher information at the beginning of the book). You can look at the copyright page in this book and use it as your guide (page 8).

Include a table of contents and an index at the back of the book. An index usually takes at least a few days to compile even on a very short book. You can pay for a professional indexing service, or you can index the book yourself. You can create your own index using Microsoft Word's indexing function. It works similar to Word's "Table of Contents" function. If you are unsure how to do this, use Microsoft Word Help, or look online.

There are lots of great books on indexing and you should try to learn as much as you can so your index looks professional. You can also hire a professional indexing service. Professional indexing typically costs about $4 per page. So, for example, if your book is 130 pages, you can expect the indexing to cost about $520. But you can negotiate. I know an excellent professional indexer that does self-published and local authors for only $2.50 per page.

If your book is a reference book, such as a medical book, it is probably best to hire a professional indexing service. If you can't afford professional indexing, purchase a book on indexing. Here are some good books on the topic:

- ***Indexing Books, Second Edition*** (Chicago Guides to Writing, Editing, and Publishing), Nancy Mulvany (I like Nancy's book the best!)
- ***The Indexing Companion***, Glenda Browne
- ***Introduction to Indexing and Abstracting***, Donald Cleveland

Professional indexing is an art and a business all to itself. The best professional indexers have analytical minds and a gift for detail. If you study indexing and you enjoy it, you may want to consider supplementing your regular writing income by offering indexing services. For more information, read the excellent article *Author as Indexer* by Madge Walls on Spawn's website (*www.spawn.org/editing/authorasindexer.htm*). If you decide to use an indexing service, use referrals from other authors or professional organizations to find a good one.

Don't try to sell your nonfiction book on CreateSpace without an index or table of contents. These two references become big selling points for your book on

Amazon. Have you ever noticed the icon at the top of the Amazon listing that says "Look Inside"?

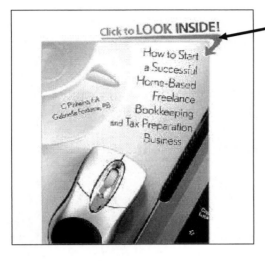

Amazon's **"Look Inside"** feature allows potential buyers to view the table of contents, the back cover, index, and a few pages of the book. A lot of books get sold this way!

Potential buyers will be able to see your index, table of contents, and a few pages of your book. It's a great marketing tool. **"Look Inside"** helps sell your book. If applicable, include a glossary and bibliography. Difficult terms and obscure language should be explained in a glossary. Quoted sources should be referenced in either footnotes, endnotes, or a bibliography. CreateSpace will make all of these book components visible in a few weeks after your book becomes available for sale on Amazon.

Even if you are on a shoestring budget, you can generate your own index, table of contents, footnotes, and bibliography in Microsoft Word. If you don't take the time to do this, your book will scream "AMATEUR!" Take the time to do it right.

7. Don't use a local print shop: get a real printer

Your local neighborhood print shop may be great at turning out letterhead, business cards, and brochures, but for books you need a specialized book printer. Unless you don't want to be taken seriously, you need a real POD printer like CreateSpace or Lulu. I suspect that more aggravation, time, and money have been lost working with printers who are not capable of turning out a professional job than in any other area of the self-publishing industry. You'll pay higher prices at the local print shop, and you may end up with an inferior product.

8. Toot your own horn!

If nobody knows about your book, nobody can purchase it. Get the word out. Send e-mails and press releases to anybody and everybody you can think of. Add a signature line to all of your e-mails with a link back to your book and your website. Send out review copies to appropriate media (more on review copies later.)

Arrange book seminars at local libraries and bookstores. Publicize that book! Promote it every day! And don't stop after that first sales surge. Find multiple ways to market your book and recycle the information in it for continued sales over the long haul. We will cover more marketing techniques later on in this book.

9. Update your website frequently

People forget things quickly, so make sure you keep your website up to date, and your book information constantly refreshed. If you have an e-mail list, use it! Always make sure your readers can contact you, either through your website, or by some other means.

I try to update my website, blog, and subsidiary websites at least once a week, and no less than once a month. If your contact information or book updates are not current, you may lose a buyer. Always make sure your information is up to date. Your next big sale may be just around the corner!

10. Get competent financial advice

Unless you have an accounting background or a close friend who does, make sure that you get competent financial advice so that you don't end up in hot water with the IRS. Spend a few hundred dollars a year on a competent tax professional. Read a few books—there are multiple resources out there specifically written for writers to help them make the most of the tax deductions that are allowed to our industry.

Meet with a CPA or an Enrolled Agent. Ask lots of questions. Trying to save a few hundred dollars by skipping a tax adviser could cost you thousands in the long run. Don't be penny-wise and pound-foolish.

Chapter 4: CreateSpace Book Basics

"Despite current weaknesses, I believe CreateSpace offers most self-publishers the best balance between convenience and profitability."

-Aaron Shepard, *Aiming at Amazon*

Book Basics

We are going to go over the basic parts of a book. You may know some of these terms already. These are definitions you must understand in order to self-publish. I recommend that you also watch the CreateSpace video tour of the book set-up process at:

www.createspace.com/Special/Help/Videos/BookTour.jsp

This will help you better understand the CreateSpace publishing process. The video tutorial is not as comprehensive as it should be, but the information is still really helpful for beginners.

A Book's Interior

There are three main parts of a book: the front matter, the body matter, and the back matter. The front matter includes the table of contents, the dedication page, the introduction, and any other parts that preface the "main part" of the book. It's basically everything before you get to the actual story.

The body matter is the actual book: the manuscript itself. The body matter may include chapters or sections.

The back matter includes all of the parts after the main part of the book. The index, epilogue, glossary, and any other sections that follow the body of the book are included in the "back matter."

A Book's Exterior

A book has a front cover, a spine, and a back cover. The spine usually includes the title, author, and publisher. The back cover usually contains the back cover blurb, which is a short description designed to sell the book. The back cover may also include the author's photo and a short bio.

LCCN Assignment

An LCCN is a Library of Congress Control Number. If you'd like to make your book available to libraries, CreateSpace can help you obtain an LCCN, so your book is given a unique identifier and is eligible for library cataloging nationwide. CreateSpace charges $75 for this service.

One caveat: An LCCN can only be assigned to books that have not been previously published. After you have approved your proof, your book is no longer eligible for this service with CreateSpace. If you plan to sell exclusively on Amazon or your website, you don't need this. But if you ever plan to sell your books to libraries, you should obtain an LCCN.

You can also go to the Library of Congress website and find out more about LCCNs. In some cases, you may be able to apply for the LCCN yourself. Go to: ***www.pcn.loc.gov*** to find out more.

Binding Choices

All the books created through the CreateSpace portal are produced as trade paperback **"perfect-bound"** books with full-color covers. You may choose a black and white or full-color interior. "Perfect binding" is a commonly used adhesive binding. Most trade paperbacks are sold with this type of binding. This binding is sometimes called a "soft cover."

Comb binding is only appropriate for cookbooks or study guides. Some bookstores will not carry books that are comb-bound. Comb binding is when the pages are punched with a machine and then inserted into a plastic "comb" that holds the pages together. The rare exception is cookbooks, which are often sold with a comb binding so the pages remain open while the reader is actually cooking. Don't try to do your own bookbinding with a comb binding system. It's just not worth the trouble. You'll save money and time by setting up your title with CreateSpace (or another POD publisher) that can produce your title professionally.

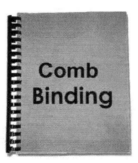

CreateSpace will allow you to print your book with a black-and-white interior, or full-color interior. As you might expect, full-color interiors cost substantially more money. The highest number of pages you can have in any trim size is 828 pages. The maximum trim size for a book with a full-color interior is 250 pages.

Hardcover books have a stiff, long-lasting cover. At the time of this book's printing, CreateSpace does not offer hardcover binding. I expect this to change soon, but if you want to publish a hardcover, you will have to use Lulu, BookSurge, or another POD printer.

Available Trim Sizes

The "trim size" of a book is the final size of a printed page when it is complete. This is the size of your final book after it is printed, bound and trimmed. Trim sizes are always indicated as width in inches by height in inches. For example, a trim size of 6" × 9" means the printed book will be 6 inches wide and 9 inches tall.[h] Mass-market paperbacks are 4" × 6.87". This size is usually associated with cheap fiction books. For nonfiction books, CreateSpace's 6" × 9" or 7" × 10" are the most suitable trim sizes. This book is a 7" × 10" trim size. All books published through CreateSpace must be a minimum of twenty-four pages (only booklets and children's books are typically this short).

Standard trim sizes (shown in **bold**) are supported with CreateSpace's excellent **Cover Creator** software, which you can use to design a professional cover for free. The maximum number of pages you can have varies by trim size and printing options.

Trim Size	Color Interior Maximum Page Count	Black & White Interior Maximum Page Count
5.25" × 8"	**250**	**828**
5.5" × 8.5"	**250**	**828**
6" × 9"	**250**	**828**
6.14" × 9.21"	250	828
6.69" × 9.61"	250	828
7" × 10"	**250**	**828**
7.44" × 9.69"	250	828
7.5" × 9.25"	250	828
8" × 10"	**250**	**440**
8.25" × 6"	**212**	**220**
8.25" × 8.25"	**212**	**220**

Again, the trim choices shown in **"bold"** allow you to use CreateSpace's cover software (which I recommend). If you already have a cover designer, you can choose any trim size you want and just upload your custom cover.

Royalty Payments from CreateSpace

CreateSpace pays your royalty for the previous month's sales at the end of the following month. For example, you will receive your royalty payment at the end of March covering all the sales you made in February. There will be a lag time of about twenty days between the close of the month and your royalty payment.

Authors living in the United States will receive royalty payments via direct deposit into their bank accounts. This service is free. By written request, a CreateSpace author can choose to be paid by check, but an $8 check fee applies.[i]

Chapter 5: How to Set Up Your Publishing Label with Bowker

"Once you have obtained your ISBNs from Bowker, you are no longer a self-publisher. You are a **publisher**—an independent publisher. There is no difference at that point between you and Random House except that Random House publishes more titles than you."

-Robert Bowie Johnson Jr., *Publishing Basics*

Setting up Your Company

This next step is to set up your publishing label with Bowker. This makes you a real publisher, because you OWN the ISBNs on your books. You have complete ownership and rights over the published material and the copyright, and you can take the book to any printer you want. This allows you complete freedom to use your material any way you wish.

Example of an ISBN and Bar Code

Purchasing an ISBN block is the cornerstone for publishing all your subsequent books. If you publish with Lulu and decide you want to publish with CreateSpace or another POD publisher, you can do it. Nobody owns the ISBN except you. By setting up your own publishing label, you will get your own block of ISBNs, which gives you full ownership of anything you publish. If you do **not** own the ISBN, you do not own all the rights to your book. Do you want to publish a foreign language edition or a large-print edition? If you own the ISBNs, you can.

Business Entity Type

Now we are going to go over some business and basic tax information. No, don't run and hide! This will only take a minute or two. Authors typically hate reading about the business side of writing, but I'll try to make this as painless as possible.

You have to decide on your business entity type in order to set up a publishing company. If you are a self-employed writer (a sole proprietor) working from your home, you can continue to be a sole proprietor when you self-publish as well.

If you are worried about liability for some reason (perhaps you publish medical books or books on legal matters) and you have the money to set up a corporation, then by all means, go see a CPA, tax attorney, or an Enrolled Agent,[j] and have him or her set up a corporate entity for you.

At the beginning, most authors just file their tax returns as a sole proprietorship. That's what I did my first two years. You can incorporate eventually. There is no definite timeline for when you should incorporate, but I firmly believe that incorporation is a good idea once your yearly profits get around $80,000-$100,000. This is just my personal opinion. You may wish to incorporate sooner. If you are concerned about any liability, you should either purchase liability insurance (enough to cover all your assets), or else consider incorporation (or both!).

Dan Poynter, author of the *Self-Publishing Manual*, says that authors should run their businesses as a sole proprietorship. Since Poynter is not an accountant, I think this is poor advice. A sole proprietorship might be fine at the beginning when you are just starting out, but once your revenues increase, so do your liabilities. Also, sole proprietorships are targeted for IRS audit 400 percent more than corporations (a sole proprietor with $100,000 in revenues will be audited at a rate of 3.9 percent, while a corporation with the same revenues will be audited at a rate of only 0.70 percent[k]—a huge difference!) For anyone who has suffered through the horror of an IRS audit, this may be reason enough to incorporate.

Now we are going to briefly review different business entity types.

Sole Proprietorship

A business controlled by one person is a sole proprietorship. A sole proprietorship is the simplest business type, and the easiest to begin and set up. It is taxed and reported on the taxpayer's personal income tax return. Income and expenses from the sole proprietorship are reported on IRS **Form 1040**, **Schedule C**: *Profit or Loss from Business.*

A sole proprietor must accept all the risks and the liabilities of the business. If a sole proprietor does not have employees, he or she generally does not have to obtain an EIN (employer identification number). You can obtain an EIN for free online on the IRS website if you don't want to use your Social Security number to identify your business.

Once you get an EIN, you can have royalty payments issued to the EIN instead of your Social Security number. Then, when you file your tax return, you file as you normally would, also including the EIN of your business on the **Schedule C**. The main reason why sole proprietors (without employees) obtain EIN numbers is for privacy reasons. If you are a sole proprietor and you hire employees, you will be required to obtain an EIN in order to issue payroll. Profits earned on a sole proprietorship are considered the income of the owner (that's you!) and are taxed as such.

Partnerships

If you regularly write with a partner, such as a husband and wife writing team, you may qualify as a partnership for tax purposes. A partnership is simply a business involving two or more owners. A partnership is NOT a corporation.

Each general partner is liable for all partnership debts regardless of participation and contribution amounts. Each partner contributes money, property, labor, or skill, and shares in the profits and losses of the business. A general partner's actions can legally bind the entire business, and general partners are legally responsible for a partnership's debts and liabilities.

Example: Billy and Jane Pratt are brother and sister. Together, they own Devil Dog Publishing. Devil Dog publishes a monthly magazine and newsletter for tattoo artists. Billy writes most of the articles and does interviews. Jane takes care of the day-to-day running of the magazine, including paying the bills and securing advertising. Billy and Jane are in a partnership.

A partnership must file an annual information return to report the income, deductions, gains, losses, etc., from its operations. Each partner includes his or her share of the partnership's income or loss on his or her tax return. Partners are **not employees** and are generally not issued W-2 forms. Partnerships file IRS **Form 1065** to report income and losses.

Partnerships are audited by the IRS at a lower rate than sole proprietorships, so if you are already writing with a partner or a spouse, you may want to report your income as a partnership in order to lower your audit risk. The IRS audits partnerships about one-half the rate of sole proprietorships.

"LLC" Limited Liability Company

A Limited Liability Company (LLC) is a relatively new business structure allowed by state statute. LLCs are popular because, similar to a corporation, owners have limited liability. An LLC is when one or more individuals form an entity with the liability protection of a corporation, but the tax benefits of a partnership.

Some financial advisers are in love with the LLC. As a rule, attorneys seem to prefer the LLC while tax professionals (such as CPAs) seem to recommend corporations. There are drawbacks and benefits to both entities. If you wish to form an LLC, seek competent legal advice.

Corporations

Unlike partnerships and sole proprietorships, corporations are considered entities separate from their owners and shareholders. A corporation is treated just like a person, with its own tax ID number (which is just like its own Social Security number) and its own separate tax return. If you form a corporation, the corporation will "pay" you as if you are a regular employee.

One of the biggest drawbacks to a corporation is the yearly tax return requirement—even if you don't have any revenues! Corporate tax returns cost money—anywhere from $500 to $3,000 a year, on average. You must file corporate tax returns EVERY SINGLE YEAR, even if you don't have any income.

If you form a corporation, you will have to pay the fees to incorporate and file yearly corporate returns whether or not you make a dime. If you fail to file corporate returns, the IRS will fine you hundreds of dollars for each failure to file. Incorporation also means that you may need to do payroll for yourself. Ouch!

Corporate tax law in the United States is very complex and beyond the scope of this book. If you want to form a corporation, get a good tax adviser to do it for you. Sit down and talk to someone about it before you do it. In many states, corporations are required to pay franchise fees in order to simply exist.

The benefits of incorporation have to do mainly with liability protection. Incorporation also helps owners manage their cash, and it shows a modicum of professionalism that a sole proprietorship does not. Incorporation also lowers your audit risk considerably. All the larger publishers are corporations. But you do not need to incorporate in order to publish.

Business Entities: PROS & CONS *Snapshot*

Type	PROS	CONS
Sole Proprietorship Schedule C	*Easiest to organize, the owner is free to make decisions, and receive all the profits *Minimum legal restrictions *Losses can offset other income	*Unlimited liability
Limited Liability Co, LLC Schedule C, Form 1065, or Form 1120S	*Disregarded entity for tax purposes *Can elect S corporation status *Multiple-member LLC defaults to partnership status *Limited liability	*Subject to Self-Employment tax *State laws can change
Partnership Form 1065	*Easy to organize *Each partner has a personal interest in the business *Pass-through entity	*Partners have unlimited liability *Authority is divided *Fringe benefits restricted
S Corporation Form 1120S	*A corporation **without** double taxation of profits *Same liability protection as a corporation *Pass-through entity *Profits passed to shareholder (s) are not subject to Self-Employment Tax	*Fringe benefits restricted *Shareholders pay as a pass-through *Limited number of shareholders
C Corporation Form 1120	*Stockholders have limited liability *There can be an unlimited number of shareholders, both foreign and domestic	*Double taxation of profits

Table information from the Internal Revenue Service website, at **www.IRS.gov**

Understanding a Writer's Realities

Running your business out of your home is definitely cheaper than having a separate commercial location. As a freelance writer, it is not necessary for you to have an office address on Main Street, USA. So that's one cost you won't have to add to your bottom line. You do get another tax break for running your business out of your house. Represented by a percentage of your entire living space, the area you allocate for your office entitles you to what is known as the Home Office Deduction.

For our purpose here, let's consider that a bonus since you would most likely have utility costs and make rent or mortgage payments for that space even if you didn't have your own business.

All businesses cost something to run. Your writing business is no different. Much of your everyday operating expense will come from the supplies you use—things like paper, envelopes, toner, software, and reference materials. There are other expenses too. If you have a separate telephone number so your kids don't answer your business calls, that will cost you a few dollars a month.

Postage and delivery costs should be factored in if you plan to send out review copies (recommended). I personally use *Stamps.com* to send out all my packages. I never have to go to the post office unless I'm sending a package overseas. *Stamps.com* costs about $15 per month, plus the cost of postage. I print out all my postage on labels and my postal carrier picks them up at my house every day. *Stamps.com* is worth the cost for the convenience of never having to stand in line at the post office with a screaming toddler on my hip. I **do** still have to stand in line when I send books overseas.

Stamps.com also allows you to ship Media Mail. Media Mail is a cheap way to mail books, DVDs, CDs, and other media (magazines do not qualify for Media Mail). Media Mail is a slower shipping method, but the cost savings is enormous when you are shipping a large number of heavy books. For example, a nine-pound box of books will ship for $5.50 using Media Mail, but can cost up to $28 using Priority Mail.

You can also print postage directly off the US Postal Service website (**www.usps.com**), but it will not allow you to print Media Mail postage labels. If you don't have the money for an online postage service, you can always go to your local post office and stand in line if you want to send packages using Media Mail service.

Business miles traveled to attend special events, workshops, and trade fairs will also add up. When calculating your cost of doing business, don't forget to include marketing and advertising costs, as well as dues to professional organizations.

If you are a part-time freelance writer, even if you have another job, you should dedicate at least ten hours a week to your writing business in order for it to be profitable. The revenue your writing generates will depend on the market and your own dedication.

Self-Publishing Changes Everything

Publishing is a very simple business. Think of it as a recipe based upon a simple mathematical equation—you buy paper for $3 a pound, printer toner for $5 a pound, mix in some free information, put the toner on the paper, and resell it for $50 a pound! I think you will agree that is a nice markup.

There was a time when self-publishing a book demanded a high investment. The minimum press run with the traditional printing process was usually somewhere around 10,000 copies, requiring an investment of several thousand dollars. Plus, you needed a lot of room to store the books when they were printed. That has all changed.[1]

Traditional publishing wasn't much better. In traditional publishing, a book's author always gets the crumbs. After the publisher, distributor, and retailer get their cut, the author is usually left with less than 5 percent of the list price, and sometimes with nothing! Publishing under your own imprint removes two of these players—the publisher and the distributor. YOU are the publisher; this results in a much larger piece of the pie for you.

When you self-publish with CreateSpace, your job is made easier. You did all the work and you wrote the book, so stop begging for the crumbs!

Trademarks and Copyrights

Let's go over copyrights and trademarks briefly. **Copyright** protects original works of authorship. A **trademark** protects words, phrases, symbols, or designs identifying the source of the goods or services. A **patent,** which is different from either of these, protects inventions or new discoveries. All of these are designed to protect intellectual property. All of these help prevent others from unlawfully copying your work.

You can **copyright** a book, article, short story, or an essay.

You can **trademark** a book series, logo, phrase, or symbol.

You can **patent** an invention, process, or machine.

See the difference?

Trademarks

My study guide series, the ***Passkey EA Review***, is a series of books about the IRS Enrolled Agent exam. The **series** is protected by a trademark. This means that, although another author may write a study guide for the Enrolled Agent exam, no one else may use the name ***"Passkey EA Review."*** You can also trademark a logo. For example, let's say your publishing company is called "Ocean Publications." If you were to adopt a custom logo of a mermaid, you could trademark your logo. You can register a trademark yourself online for $275 at:

www.uspto.gov

I attempted to trademark my company logo and because of a technical error, my trademark application was rejected. In the end, I ended up using a trademark attorney to sort out the mess. If you decide to use an attorney, you will pay about $500-$800 per trademark, plus the filing fees. A good attorney will also do a thorough search and let you know if a similar trademark is already in use. For me, it was worth it. I just don't have the time or the expertise to deal with legal matters, and I thought the cost was reasonable. My trademark attorney is:

Lee, Lee and Associates^m
2531 Jackson Road Ste 234
Ann Arbor, MI 48103
Phone: 1-866-400-2507
E-mail: tm@llapc.com

They specialize entirely in trademark law. They always respond to my e-mails within twenty-four hours. You can also search the Internet for a trademark service—some companies will fill the paperwork out for you for a fee.

Copyrights

All my books are protected by copyright. You are automatically granted copyright when you produce your book. Copyright exists from the moment the work is created. The copyright protection is automatic. However, you may prefer to **register** your copyright with the U.S. Copyright Office.

Registration is voluntary. Authors may choose to register their works because they want their work to be registered in the public record and have a certificate of registration. You must register your work before you bring a lawsuit for copyright infringement.[n] An online registration of an original work of authorship costs $35 at the U.S. Copyright Office website. Go to:

www.copyright.gov/register

U.S. law protects your copyright until seventy years after your death. If you want to know more about copyright law and how to register your copyright, consider purchasing Nolo Press's excellent book, *The Copyright Handbook: What Every Writer Needs to Know.* It will show you how to register a copyright for your book. The book also goes over the "fair use" doctrine, which is a sticky part of copyright law that all authors should understand.

Get Your Own ISBNs

The ISBN is the number that identifies you (and your company) as the publisher of your book. Once you purchase the ISBN and assign it to your book, you can change printers, wholesalers, and anything else about the distribution of the book. You own the entire process. Therefore, you also control the profit.

To obtain your own ISBNs, the first step is to go to the Bowker website *(www.bowker.com).* Bowker is the official ISBN agency for the United States. It is exclusively responsible for the assignment of the ISBN prefix to publishers in the U.S. If you want to sell your book through major book retailers, wholesalers, distributors, and multiple sales channels, you need an ISBN.

Major retailers and bookselling channels including Amazon, Barnes & Noble, and Borders, as well as libraries and their respective bibliographic databases, require an ISBN to identify both the title of the book and the publisher.

ISBNs help consumers find books, facilitate price comparisons, and find nearest locations to borrow books from libraries. Bowker keeps track of all the ISBNs that have been assigned to publishers and their books. At the time of this printing, ISBNs were priced as follows:
- A single ISBN: $125
- 10 Block: $250.00
- 100 Block: $575.00
- 1,000 Block: $1,000.00

Your ISBNs never expire. You will be able to use the ISBNs as you write your books, even if it takes many years. However, you can never re-use the same

ISBN. Different book editions, such as a paperback, hardcover, or Kindle edition will all be assigned their own ISBN, so if you plan to publish multiple editions of the same book, you will need multiple ISBNs in order to distinguish the different editions from one another.

Take a few hours, at a minimum, navigating all the websites Bowker has to offer. Bowker's main website is difficult to navigate, but after a while, you'll learn the ropes and understand how to get the information you need.

Next is a look at the ISBN application process, step-by-step.

Step 1: Go to www.myidentifiers.com

This is the website where you begin the process for getting your ISBNs. *www.myidentifiers.com* is a Bowker website, not a middleman or an intermediary company that charges you to obtain ISBNs on your behalf. Bowker offers many options for self-published authors, including the ability to purchase just a single ISBN. I do not recommend purchasing a single ISBN.

The reason being is the cost of a single ISBN is $125. Consequently, you will only be able to publish one book. The cost of *ten* ISBNs (this is also called an ISBN "block") will cost you about $250, which is $25 each. Having the additional ISBNs is a necessity if you are going to publish multiple versions of your book, or publish derivative works such as e-books or an expanded edition. Those ten ISBNs will go fast, trust me!

At the time of this printing, CreateSpace was offering authors the opportunity to publish their books using a free ISBN. This may seem like a good idea at first, but remember that the ISBN CreateSpace assigns you *belongs* to CreateSpace, not to you! This means that CreateSpace is the "imprint of record" through distribution channels, and CreateSpace will be listed as the publisher. Since this whole book is about how to form your own publishing company, why would you give all that up for a measly $25?

Buy your own ISBNs. Own your own publishing company. Keep all your rights. It's that simple.

Step 2: Apply for an ISBN Prefix

Once you go to **www.myidentifiers.com**, click on the link that allows you to apply for an ISBN prefix. This is for a permanent registration of a block of ISBNs. Once you buy the numbers, they **belong to you**. The ISBNs will be assigned to your publishing company as publisher of record. Each number within your prefix can then be assigned to uniquely identify the title throughout the supply chain. At the time of this printing, the cheapest block is an ISBN block of ten, which will cost you $250. This will give you the right to publish ten books or book derivatives (such as an e-book or a large-print edition) using any self-publishing method you wish.

Click on the link that says "Buy Now." This allows you to create a new account. Next you will be asked to enter your company information. You will fill out all your personal and company information. Remember when I told you to pick a name for your publishing company? Well, here's your chance to use it! Then add your e-mail and your password. Complete the web-form and submit it.

Step 3: Don't Purchase Bar Codes, Just the ISBNs

You will be taken to the next step, where you will be asked to purchase bar codes. Bowker gives you the option to purchase "EAN Bar Codes" or a "bar code graphic symbol," which is basically the scannable image that goes on the back of your books.

You don't need to purchase bar codes if you publish with CreateSpace! CreateSpace will format your bar codes on the back of your book for free. Hit "continue."

Even if you choose to publish with a company other than CreateSpace, you don't need to buy barcodes! If you publish with Lulu or any other major POD publisher, their computer software will automatically format the bar codes for you on the back of the book. Save your money—just buy the ISBNs. You can always go back and purchase the "EAN Bar Code" later if you really need it.

> Don't be fooled! You don't need to purchase "bar codes." CreateSpace will format the bar codes for you for free!

(Bookland EAN bar code graphic symbol)
EAN Bar Code—CreateSpace will format your bar code *FOR FREE*
when you submit your book for publishing!

Next, you will be taken to a screen where you can pay for your ISBNs. That's it! You are now the proud owner of your own publisher's block of ISBNs.

Step 4: Submit Your Book Title to BowkerLink™

After you receive your new ISBNs, you will need to assign your book to the particular ISBN you have chosen. If you haven't written your book yet, or if you are still deciding on a title, just come back and do this step when you are ready to publish your book.

Once you have decided on your title and cover image, you can submit your title information at ***BowkerLink***. BowkerLink is an online portal where publishers can submit their titles and post them on the Bowker database.

This free portal allows you to list your titles through Bowker, which basically means that your title will be listed in the universal database "Books in Print." After your title becomes listed on BowkerLink, it can be seen by many sectors of the book industry including wholesalers, distributors, retail chains, independent retailers, online retailers, schools, libraries, and universities.

Once you add a title on BowkerLink, it becomes assigned to your publishing company and you can upload images of the cover. Sometimes this takes a few days. You may also view and update your publisher contact information. The good part about this website is that if you make a mistake, you can always go in and update your title later.

Since CreateSpace is not technically a book distributor, BowkerLink will be for information only. It gives retailers, libraries, and other outlets a way to contact you if they want information about buying your book.

Don't be discouraged by the fact that you may not see your book in bookstores. As Aaron Shepard says, "Forget bookstores!" The reality is that most bookstores don't carry self-published authors anyway, and your best bet will be marketing directly on the biggest bookstore in the world—namely, Amazon. The easiest path to success on Amazon is by using CreateSpace.

Chapter 6: Submitting Your Manuscript

"Unlike fiction books, readers purchase nonfiction books for one of two reasons: (1) to solve a problem or (2) to achieve a goal."

-Roger C. Parker, Author

Publishing with CreateSpace

Now we are going to assume that you have at least a rough draft of your book. If you don't, get going already! You have to get your book written before you go any further.

Most successful nonfiction books are put together quickly. Most surveys report that nonfiction authors take between four to twelve months to produce a manuscript. This varies by industry and subject matter. If yours takes longer, that's okay. And if you produced your manuscript faster, that doesn't necessarily mean that it's not marketable.

Dan Poynter, the self-publishing guru, reports that he put together his bestselling book, *"Hang Gliding,"* in less than thirty days and had the book published within four months. So far, *Hang Gliding* has sold more than 130,000 copies. ° Not bad for thirty days of work!

Readers purchase nonfiction because they want valuable information on a particular subject. You don't need to write an epic. Your book should be concise, informational, and easy to read. You're the expert; you have the knowledge. A good copy editor can help you with the other stuff. Set aside time each day to write. This is an investment in your future and yourself.

Hiring a Copy Editor

Your book is written and proofread, by you. Now you need a copy editor. If you have a friend who works in the field of English such as a teacher or a fellow writer, you could ask him or her to do the editing. But hiring a freelance copy editor is not that expensive and is absolutely necessary if you want to be taken seriously. (I learned this the HARD way by seeing my own typos pointed out by book buyers.) Now I never publish anything without the help of a copy editor. While this doesn't preclude the possibility of errors, it reduces the chance that your book will be mocked for spelling and syntax errors.

A copy editor is essential if English is not your primary language, or if you don't have a lot of writing experience. Your editor can also provide valuable feedback and suggestions on how to improve your book. Ask your editor to tell you what he or she likes or dislikes about the manuscript. Ask how you might improve it. LISTEN. Don't fall in love with your book.

You want to produce a product that's useful, and feedback from your editor provides a great opportunity to make your book better. You could write your book and publish it without using a copy editor, but I strongly recommend against this. The easiest way to find a copy editor is online.

I use **Craigslist,** a free online classified site (***www.craigslist.com***). I created a free account and I use it to post my copy editor jobs. It's free to post freelance jobs in the "gigs" section of Craigslist.

Typically, I describe the project and word count, and set a maximum price for the job. An experienced copy editor will generally charge between $20 and $65 per hour. I usually post a rate of $25 per hour and receive dozens of responses. Some are unprofessional, and I delete these.

I always get at least five to ten responses from experienced copy editors willing to do the job at a reasonable price. If you can't afford much, then post the most you are willing to pay—be **honest** (for example, $150), and say that the gig is perfect for an English student or a retired teacher. You'll get responses right away, trust me.

If the respondent has obvious spelling and syntax errors in their resume or their e-mail, just delete it. A person who doesn't take the time to spell-check their own e-mails is not going to do a great job as a copy editor. Post your e-mail address (not your phone number) in the ad, and have respondents send you a resume or other information that you'd like to see. Here are a few sample ads:

Sample Ad #1

Small publishing company seeks a copy editor for a new book, 125 pages (word count 30,000) on home brewing. This gig pays a maximum of $150, one half up-front and the other half upon delivery of the manuscript. This is a great gig for a retired teacher or English student. Please e-mail your qualifications to the address below: *BeerMaker@yahoo.com*

Sample Ad #2

Innovative new publisher seeks a copy editor for a new book, 245 pages (word count 56,000). The book is about petunia gardening, so we prefer someone with some industry experience. Pay is $35 per hour up to a maximum of $600. Experienced copy editors only! Please e-mail: *FlowerPubs@gmail.com*

When you pick out respondents that you like, e-mail them a few sample pages and ask them to edit those. Then make your decision based on that. The next step after the editing process is the submission of your manuscript.

Submitting Your PDF File to CreateSpace

Now that your manuscript is written and professionally copyedited, here's the next step. Let's set up your title with CreateSpace. CreateSpace will allow you to distribute your book on Amazon.com and your own website without any setup fees or inventory. Start at:

www.CreateSpace.com.

1. Create a free CreateSpace account

If you don't already have an account, create one now. Fill out the short form on the webpage. Membership is free, and it only takes a few minutes to sign up. Once you log in, you will need to provide information such as your bank account routing number so you can receive your royalties, and all of your shipping, billing, and account preferences. You can make changes later, if necessary, by using the links at the bottom of the page.

CreateSpace is a free service. It offers limited phone support, and even its e-mail support is spotty. It takes about forty-eight hours for support personnel to answer your e-mail—you'll probably have figured it out on your own by the time they get back to you. I am hoping that this will change eventually— the only area where CreateSpace is lacking is customer service. It's not designed for someone who is computer-illiterate.

But CreateSpace is the best option for anyone who wants to self-publish for FREE. The instructions below should help you set up your title with a minimum of fuss, but if you get lost or confused, go to the CreateSpace "Help" pages and read up a bit, or start over from step one.

Once you get used to navigating CreateSpace's website, you will love its ease of use and completely automated features. If you require more technical support, book design, and author's services, you should try using Amazon's BookSurge instead. BookSurge can format and edit your interior files for a fee. And it isn't cheap! Realize that you will pay a premium for all those service extras!

2. Set up your book title

To add a book, log in to your member account and add your new title. To start the process, click on the icon to set up a book. You will be asked to provide required information such as book title, author name, page count, trim size, etc. Do not forget to enter a description of your book in the space provided to help entice readers to take a closer look. If you want to set up a CD or a DVD, you can do that too.

Be careful when you choose the wording of your title. Try to be descriptive. Short titles are easier to remember, but keywords are important these days because they help your buyer find your book. Some believe that a short, concise title is better, but I believe that a longer, descriptive title will help readers find your book on Amazon and other search engines.

Before you choose a title, do numerous keyword searches and find books on similar subject matter. Research other titles on Amazon. Examine those titles and their cover art. Make sure that your book looks different—you don't want to publish a book with an identical title or similar cover art. Use your competitors' books as a guideline for how you should format and title your own book.

Don't use the exact title that anyone else has. You can't copyright a title, which is why you'll often see books with identical titles. Although librarians and bookstore owners search for books using an ISBN, book BUYERS rarely search for books under ISBNs. They search for titles, authors, and subject matter.

Don't use an obscure title or one with intentionally misspelled words—no one will be able to find it! Use keywords that you might use to find similar books. This is the key to getting your book found by buyers. Make sure your title is descriptive enough that it will come up in multiple keyword searches. Avoid clichés like "Best" or "Most." These words won't help buyers find your book in keyword searches.

> "The overriding goal of successful nonfiction is to communicate the benefit that readers will enjoy as simply as possible."
> **-Roger C. Parker, Author**

Your title should offer a promise or communicate a **benefit** to the buyer. Your subtitle reinforces the main title, preferably with additional keywords that help drive buyers to your Amazon listing. Nonfiction sells better if the title features a "highly obvious" benefit.

Let's look at an example. Try searching for the word "Money" on Amazon. One of the first books to pop up is *The Total Money Makeover: A Proven Plan for Financial Fitness,* by Dave Ramsey. This is an example of a title that offers a promise to the buyer. It also utilizes great keywords. A potential buyer that searches for "Money" or "Financial Plan" is going to find this book. The subject matter of the book should be obvious at first glance. Choose your title wisely; it will be with your book forever. A good title can even be a jumping off point for an entire brand.

As you set up your book on CreateSpace, you can make editorial and cover changes until the point you submit the book for publishing. Once you submit the book for publishing, you will be required to order a "proof copy" of the book.

A proof is a copy of the book for you to review before the title is finalized. Proofs are normally shipped within five business days. After you receive the proof, review it. If you want to make corrections, you can do so.

If you are unhappy with your proof, (or you find errors) you will be able to correct your original manuscript and upload a new PDF file to CreateSpace. A CreateSpace employee will review your PDF to make sure the formatting is okay, and then you will be asked if you want to proceed. At this point, you will have to order another proof. You can repeat these steps as many times as you like until you get a proof that you are happy with. So nothing is set in stone at this point—don't worry. You can still make changes!

The next step is to fill out the ISBN. Fill out your "imprint name" (this is the name of your publishing company). You will be asked to choose a "category" for your book. CreateSpace is asking you to choose the general subject of your book, such as business, art, fiction, or reference. You may not find your exact "category" for your book, so just do your best to find a category that is similar and move on. If you can't find a category that applies to your book, you should look at similar books on Amazon and see how they are categorized.

After you have filled out the title information, you will be asked to enter in some keywords or "tags" for your book. Enter in basic keywords for your title—the words that a buyer might use when they are searching for a book on the same subject. CreateSpace will only let you enter three or four keywords, but don't worry about this—when the book is listed on Amazon, you can manually add tags, and in a few months, Amazon's search engines will automatically search the book for keywords and post them to the listing.

The rest of the title set-up is pretty self-explanatory. Add your pen name as the author's name. Your copyright date will be set automatically—it is the date you approve your book as final.

3. Formatting your interior files

This next step takes you to where you can fill out your page count and trim size (the size of the pages in the book). Professional book formatting is expensive, and can range from a few hundred to a few thousand dollars per book. There are numerous professional software suites that are designed to help authors format their book's interior. The most popular book formatting software is *Adobe InDesign* or *QuarkXPress*.

If you cannot afford either of these programs, you can format your book in Microsoft Word. There are numerous "how to" websites that can show you how to format a book in Microsoft Word, based on the trim size that you want to use. With a smaller trim size, you may have to get professional formatting, or set the margins smaller and CreateSpace will adjust the PDF so that it will be centered.

If you want to do it all yourself, purchase Aaron Shepard's book, *Perfect Pages*. He will show you how to format your book in Microsoft Word and how to prepare it for publication. There is no book on the market that covers book formatting in Microsoft Word as well as *Perfect Pages*. *Perfect Pages* covers Microsoft Word 97-2003 for Windows, and Word 2004 for the Mac.

There is some updated information for Word 2007 and 2008 on Aaron Shepard's excellent website. If you want to attempt really fancy formatting or an exotic trim size, purchase *Perfect Pages* and learn how to do it right. Check out Aaron Shepard's website, ***www.newselfpublishing.com***. There's a lot of great information there. Shepard is also the author of *Aiming at Amazon*, a popular book about how to sell exclusively through Amazon. Both of his books are essential reading for any author who wants to self-publish.

Complete formatting techniques are beyond the scope of this book (that would take another 200 pages). But you can still publish using CreateSpace's largest trim size (8 **x** 10) with a minimum of fuss, since 8 **x** 10 is very close to a standard page. On a side note, Lulu actually offers a trim size that is identical to a standard sheet of paper, so you don't have to do anything to get the interior file to format correctly.

4. Super Simple Book Formatting

If you know how to use Adobe Acrobat and Microsoft Word, then it will be easy for you to format your book to the appropriate trim size. You will need to convert your formatted Word document to a PDF in order to submit the title to CreateSpace for publishing.

It's not that difficult to figure out how to set up Word and Adobe Acrobat for special page sizes. After purchasing Shepard's book, *Perfect Pages*, I was able to format my own books in custom trim sizes in about a week.

For CreateSpace, the easiest trim size to format is 8 × 10. This is the closest size to a standard sheet of paper, so you don't have to do much in Microsoft Word to get the interior file to fit within the trim size. If you want to use the simplest formatting, set your manuscript margins at about 1.4" all around. Then choose the 8 × 10 trim size.

You will then need to convert your manuscript to PDF. You do this by printing your manuscript to a PDF converter, such as Adobe Acrobat. If you keep your margins at between 1.3-1.5", your converted PDF file will fit within CreateSpace's 8 × 10 trim size. This will leave plenty of room for your text to be legible and for the book to print correctly. The book will be a large trade paperback.

You can choose another basic trim size, such as 6 × 9, by going to the page set-up screen in Microsoft Word. Do this by going to the Microsoft Word **"File"** drop-down menu. Select **File > Page Setup > Paper,** and change the width and height. For example, if you have chosen a 6 × 9 paperback, then you can change your "paper size" to **A5**, which is a height of 8.27" and a width of 5.83". The size "A5" is the name of the paper size using the **international paper size standard.**

Here's an important note about postage. A shorter book, say a 150-page 6 × 9 book, will fit easily into a smaller envelope, and weighs about ten ounces. This means that shipping will still qualify for First-Class mail, which is fast and cheap. Anything LESS THAN thirteen ounces may ship First-Class. Consider your postage costs if your book is anywhere from 150-200 pages.

Many authors do not think about weight while they are publishing a book, but it's significant. Weigh your book when the proof comes in. Is the weight very close to a pound? Consider some editing changes or getting rid of some superfluous pages, if you can.

Postage costs are often overlooked when authors are planning their book release. But having a book that is under thirteen ounces versus fourteen ounces will double your postage costs. This will increase your costs a great deal if you plan to send out review copies. Or it will force you to use Media Mail, which is much slower.

This book is formatted to CreateSpace's 7 X 10 trim size. If you go into Microsoft Word and select **File > Page Setup > Paper**, you can set your manuscript to a 7 X 10 trim size by selecting **B5** (this is the **international paper size** for a 7 X 10 trim size). Just make sure you save an original copy of your manuscript so that you can go back to it. This is just in case you do something that you can't reverse.

You can **format** your entire manuscript in Microsoft Word, but ultimately you will need to submit your manuscript in PDF format. **Adobe Acrobat** is the program that creates PDF files (not to be confused with **Adobe READER**, a free program that allows you to *read* PDF files, but not actually create them).

Adobe Acrobat's logo looks like this.

Once you *create* your PDF file, the icon will look like this.

You cannot upload a manuscript in Microsoft Word to CreateSpace. All files must be submitted as PDFs through CreateSpace's website portal (this is a lot easier than it sounds, trust me!). The interior file for your book should not exceed 100 MB. If your book has a color interior or multiple photographs, you may exceed this file size limit. If your interior files are all black and white, you should be fine.

If you do not own Adobe Acrobat and you cannot afford to purchase it, you can download a free PDF "converter" that will create a PDF file from your Microsoft Word manuscript. The most popular free PDF converter software is **PrimoPDF**. This free software tool for PDF creation can be downloaded at: *www.primopdf.com.*

PrimoPDF doesn't do a great job on photographs, but if your book is all black-and-white text, it works just fine. If your book contains photographs, you should purchase Adobe Acrobat; otherwise, the image quality won't be very good.

If all else fails, you can hire a book designer to format your book. If you aren't sure you can do it yourself, or if you've been told the interior looks "amateurish," then you might want to invest in professional interior book design. CreateSpace offers design packages, but these are rather expensive.

Kindle Formatting

For Kindle and e-book formatting, I recommend **eBook Architects** (don't try to do Kindle formatting yourself unless you know how to link within an e-document—Kindle readers get very upset if their e-books are not formatted correctly and they WILL leave bad reviews).

The contact information for **eBook Architects** is:

eBook Architects
512-939-3466
www.ebookarchitects.com

If you want to attempt your own Kindle formatting, you can purchase Joshua Tallent's excellent book, *Kindle Formatting: The Complete Guide To Formatting Books For The Amazon Kindle*. The book has great reviews, but it's not designed for a newbie, so don't expect to understand the complexities unless you have some existing computer knowledge.

If you decide to use a professional formatter, call around and get some price quotes. Also, don't be afraid to tell book designers what your budget is—see if they will work with you. It never hurts to ask.

5. Choosing a Font

Don't use more than two different fonts in your manuscript. The primary font should be a nice, legible *serif* font, like the ones shown next:

Garamond,
Baskerville,
Georgia
Goudy, or
Bookman

Many self-published authors use Times New Roman because it is the default font in Microsoft Word. Times New Roman is not an ideal font for books because it was actually designed for newspaper use. Most traditional publishers do not use Times New Roman as the font for their books. Try to avoid using

Times New Roman if you can. Do not use Courier, *cursive* font, or any type of cartoony font. Your chapter headings can be a nice *sans-serif* font like **Arial**. Serif fonts have little tails at the end of each letter.

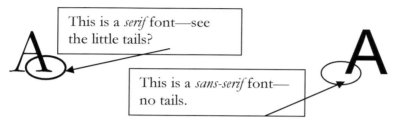

This is a *serif* font—see the little tails?

This is a *sans-serif* font—no tails.

If you use too many fonts, the manuscript will look sloppy. Don't use a font size that's too large (unless the book is a large-print book), and don't use a tiny font either. A 12-point font is usually good, with a larger font size for the chapter headings. With the exception of children's books, anything larger than 12-point font is considered a "large-print" edition.

When you convert the manuscript to PDF format, you will have to set the page size to match your trim size, as well. I use Adobe Acrobat software to convert my PDF files. Experiment with your PDF software. Try converting your manuscript to multiple page sizes. Then you can choose the trim size that you like best.

If you are unsure of the trim size you want to use, but you still want to set up your title and play with the Cover Creator, just guess at the page count, and choose any trim size. That will allow you to play with CreateSpace's other book design features. You can always change the page count and trim size later if you want. But you cannot order your proof until your page numbers and trim size are chosen.

Make sure your manuscript has page numbers. This may seem obvious, but it is often forgotten by beginners. In Word, go to **Insert>Page Numbers**. Don't put a page number on the first page.

6. Prepare and upload your manuscript

The next step is to prepare and upload your completed manuscript. When you are ready, upload your book's interior files to your CreateSpace member account. Make sure your pages are all numbered in sequential order. Microsoft

Word will allow you to re-start the numbering of your pages in the middle of a document. I know, because I have done this *on accident!*

If your pages are not numbered correctly in sequential order, CreateSpace will reject your manuscript. CreateSpace will not tell you exactly where the problem is—you will only receive a vague e-mail about the manuscript having unacceptable pagination. This is another one of CreateSpace's shortcomings. In order to take advantage of their super-cheap printing services, you have to figure a lot of this stuff out for yourself.

7. Design your cover

CreateSpace's free online cover generator, Cover Creator, is GREAT. Cover Creator is easy to use—you just go through the steps, one by one. You can design a beautiful cover yourself using this software. But don't be lazy. Try to be thoughtful when creating your cover.

A cover WILL make or break your book. Take time to experiment with your cover. It took a few weeks of experimentation and numerous cover photos before we settled on the cover for this book. People buy with their eyes, and attention to detail should go into your cover. Your book's cover **is not** an afterthought.

Don't use cursive fonts or strange lettering. Make sure your title and subtitle are legible and clear. Remember that your book will be viewed as a "thumbnail" (a very small image) on Amazon, and the busier your cover, the less clear your title will be. Don't use a diagram on the cover. Don't use tiny pictures on your cover. No one will be able to see them on the Amazon listing page.

Do not use the stock photos that CreateSpace uses on the sample covers. This seems obvious, but I saw a book listed on Amazon recently where the author hadn't bothered to change the CreateSpace stock photo. Her book looked terrible. Don't let your cover become the butt of someone's joke.

You will need to decide whether or not to use an author's photo. Unless you're famous, don't use your own photo on the front cover. If you use your photo for the back cover, be cautious about the picture that you choose. Remember that buyers have a lot of prejudices even if they don't admit them. I don't use an author's photo on my accounting and tax-related books.

Even if you decide not to use an author's photo on your books, you will need one eventually. If you don't have a nice professional photograph, ask a friend to use a digital camera to take a picture of you on a white or neutral background. Put on a nice sweater or shirt and make sure it's not busy with crazy patterns. If you're unsure about the color, just wear black. Smile. Make your photo friendly and inviting. Your readers are your extended family—they should enjoy seeing your picture. If you don't want to use an author's photo, then don't.

Purchase nice stock photography. You don't have to spend a fortune, but always make sure your photos are high quality. For all of my books, I have purchased good stock photos from an online photography provider. The photos cost about $10. Here are some popular stock photo providers:

- **www.dreamstime.com:** This one is my favorite—their stock photography can't be beat, and they also let you download really nice free photos—just check their website once a week and see the new ones that photographers post. I like Dreamstime because you can purchase a single image without having to sign up for lots of other extras.

- **www.iStockphoto.com:** Another good stock photo provider.

- **www.GettyImages.com:** This stock photo company lets you choose the content that you'd like to search for, such as business or creative. Their photo database includes images of famous people and celebrities.

Play around with the Cover Creator for at least a few days. Try different fonts and photos. Ask friends and family which cover they like the best. Take their opinions under advisement. Remember, the cover has to appeal to your customer, not to you. And make sure your copy editor or proofreader looks at the cover too.

Did you know that cover typos are one of the most common mistakes that self-published authors make? A cover typo could cost you a lot of money, especially if you order a large number of books for your own use or to send out to reviewers.

Avoid a cover or a title that doesn't translate well. Your book will be sold globally on Amazon, and some words don't translate well for overseas audiences. Did you know that "rubber" is a common name for an eraser in England? In the United States, it's slang for a condom. Most of these irregularities between American and British English are innocuous. But sometimes the language differences backfire on authors.

Always e-mail a copy of your cover to your copy editor. I did this, and sure enough, she found a typo. I had placed two periods at the end of a sentence. She caught the mistake in time, before I even ordered my proof.

8. Compose your back cover copy

You will also need to decide on your back cover copy. Potential buyers always read the back cover description. Read examples of other successful authors' back cover descriptions—they are always short, to the point, and include a "hook."

A "hook" is a unique selling point that is designed to make the customer curious about your book and want to buy it. The back cover should offer a promise or clearly explain a benefit that the consumer will receive.

You may want to add a testimonial or review to the back. You can include a brief author's bio (information about you) on the back too.

Make sure that you run a spell-check on your back cover text. It is a good idea to paste directly from Word after you have double-checked the spelling. Once you have prepared your cover and back cover copy, you need to decide on a price for your book. Here is an example of the back cover copy for one of our bookkeeping titles:

Back Cover Copy (example)

Learn how to open your own bookkeeping business in 30 days! These ideas and techniques show you how to quickly build a flourishing full-time or part-time home-based bookkeeping or tax practice, and keep it running profitably. Some of the topics covered in this volume:

- How to get started and obtain all necessary business licenses
- How to manage your cash flow for maximum profitability and business success
- How to attract the most profitable clients
- How to increase referrals
- How to set and collect your fees
- How to offer tax services to your existing clients

And much, much more!

See how the **promise** is clearly explained? Buyers want to know what your book can do for **them**!

9. Pricing your book

Pricing your book on CreateSpace is as easy as entering in a number. You just pick a list price and that's it, right? Wrong. This section is designed to assist you in figuring out how much you can charge for your book.

Once you decide to self-publish, one of the most difficult decisions is figuring out what to charge for your book. It is natural to want to see just how much money you can make writing. So how much can you charge for your book?

The answer is: there are no set rules about pricing. Sorry!

You may think that you will attract more buyers by keeping your list prices low. But you won't be making much money and you'll be exhausted for your efforts. I consistently see self-published authors price their books way below similar books already on the market. When you set your pricing, charge according to the value of the material you produce.

One of the most common pitfalls for new writers is undervaluing their product. Charge a fair amount for what you provide from the very beginning. Value what you produce, and your readers will too.

If you don't want to make any money, there are plenty of volunteer organizations that are in desperate need of your help! If you don't care about making a profit, then volunteer work will be far more satisfying than running your own business.

All you really have to sell is your time, that is, the time it takes to create a sellable piece of writing. The level of skill needed to complete the work should be reflected in your list price. That is a good reason to charge different rates for different types of books, but ultimately it all comes down to what you are able to accomplish in a given amount of time. All writing takes time, no matter how efficient or skilled you are. How much do you value your precious time? This is the question that all new writers face.

Retail margin is the difference between a book's wholesale price and the book's retail price. The difference between the two is the profit earned by the book's retailer. Don't ever forget that you are offering an important service and charge accordingly. **Retail price** is the same as cover price, selling price, or list price.

When you self-publish, you are able to keep a larger portion of the book's **retail price** for yourself. That doesn't mean that you should price your book "down" in order to make it cheaper than all your competitors.

On the contrary, you should instead try to find a **median price** based on similar books already on the market. Don't ever be the cheapest! Readers will assume that your book isn't "as good" as a more expensive one. It's a well-known marketing fact that customers often equate lower prices with inferior quality products, and vice versa.

When you self-publish, the best way to price your book is to examine the pricing of your competitors. That way, you will know if you are pricing your book appropriately for the market.

Never undercut all of your competition. But also try to avoid being the most expensive book on the market unless your book is a textbook. Try to find a reasonable median price. It will be easy to do the research.

Spend a few hours on the Internet and Amazon. Find books with similar subject matter and check their page count. Amazon allows buyers to read excerpts from many of their listings. Shop local bookstores and look at similar books. If you can read an excerpt from your competitors' books, do so. This will help you to better understand your competition.

After you finish your research, create your own spreadsheet and list comparable titles with their retail prices. It will give you a clear indication of where you might want to set the retail price for your own book. Make reasonable adjustments for page count.

Dan Poynter, as well as a number of other self-published authors, advises that you should price your book between five to eight times the publication cost. So, for example, if your book costs you $2.50 each, the list price should be at least $12.50.

Poynter's formula does not apply to e-books or Kindle titles. This is a basic guideline to follow, but I still think it is better to use competitive titles as a guideline for pricing. Your price will vary based on the subject matter.

A 200-page scholarly book aimed at doctors or attorneys may be priced at $100. A 200-page book about gift baskets may be priced at $15. Never forget the audience you are writing for and what they expect.

Remember, you may have started writing because you love it, but this is a business, and in order to be successful, you have to make money. Do not under-price your book, and do not over-price it either.

Real-Life Book Pricing Example

In January 2009, our company published a book called **"How to Start a Successful Home-Based Freelance Bookkeeping and Tax Preparation Business."** It was a niche book, designed for home-based bookkeepers and tax preparers. That was our audience. When attempting to price the book, we looked at all the other current titles on the market with similar subject matter.

$ 39.95

Competitors' Titles	**List Price**
Successful QuickBooks Consulting	$24.95
Getting Started in Tax Consulting	$34.95
Building a Profitable Online Accounting Practice	$39.95
Starting and Building Your Own Accounting Business	$50.00
How To Open Your Own In-Home Bookkeeping Service	$59.95

Using the above information, we set the target price for our book at $39.95. We sold our first copy on Amazon within thirty days of submitting the book for publication on CreateSpace. The book was moderately successful right away, and continues to generate a nice steady income for us every single month, without any promotion or marketing other than the listing on our regular website.

10. Wait for your file to be reviewed by CreateSpace

Once your book is set up in the system and you have prepared your cover and interior files, CreateSpace will review your PDF file to make sure it complies with their submission requirements. This usually takes about twenty-four hours, and you will not be able to upload revised files or edit your book's information during this time. Someone at CreateSpace will check the manuscript for formatting issues, and if your PDF has really bad formatting problems (like the words "bleed" outside the trim size), they will e-mail you and tell you that you need to fix your interior file.

Don't panic when you can't access your manuscript! While CreateSpace is reviewing your interior files, you will not be able to access your book or make any changes. Once the review is complete, you will be notified of the results via e-mail. If your files meet CreateSpace's specifications, you may move on to the next step in the bookmaking process, ordering your proof. You may also choose to fix errors and re-submit your manuscript.

CreateSpace will NOT check your manuscript for grammar errors or formatting mistakes! This is *your* job. So make sure that you edit your book before you present it to CreateSpace for review.

11. Order a proof

After your book has been reviewed by CreateSpace, you will receive an e-mail with additional instructions. Once your PDF has been approved for printing, you will need to order a proof to make sure you are satisfied with the final product. You will be prompted for your shipping and billing address. The cost for a proof copy is the same as for a wholesale copy of your book.

Your proof will arrive at your home in about five to fourteen days, depending on the shipping method you choose. When the proof copy arrives, read it cover to cover and check it for errors. Check your title and back cover text to make sure there are no errors. This is an excellent time for your copy editor to do one final check as well.

One last time, make sure you have a trusted friend or colleague look it over. Don't be offended if they tell you it's difficult to understand or there are parts that are unclear. This is good criticism—if you can correct any problems before your book hits Amazon, you have a better chance of making it a real hit!

After you receive the proof, correct any mistakes in your manuscript. Use a red pen or a highlighter and read through the entire manuscript. Clearly mark any errors.

If you find mistakes in the proof, here is your chance to correct them. Go into your title (on your CreateSpace Dashboard) and upload a new, updated PDF copy of your manuscript. You will be required to wait about 24 hours while CreateSpace reviews the new PDF for formatting issues.

You will then be required to order a new proof in order to review it. Continue to order and correct your proofs until you have a book that you're proud of.

Make sure you are happy with all aspects of the book. If you are unhappy with the proof or you find errors, you can edit your title, upload new interior files, and order a new proof.

12. Last step—submit your proof as final!

You're at the end of the road! You've received your proof, reviewed it for errors, and now it's perfect! Make sure your price is exactly what you want, and double-check the ISBN. The last step is to submit the title for publication. Take a deep breath. You're almost done!

You can now activate your title. To do this, click the "Approve Proof" button on your member account. **Click!** Your CreateSpace e-store will activate immediately. Your Amazon.com detail page will become live within fifteen business days.

CreateSpace says that it can take up to six weeks for your book to show up on Amazon (although I have found that the listing happens much faster). In the meantime, work on your website, market your book on the web, and purchase author's copies (which you can order dirt-cheap on CreateSpace), so you can send out copies to your friends, family, and to potential reviewers.

From this day forward, you will use your CreateSpace "Dashboard" to manage all your titles and review sales and royalties. The CreateSpace Dashboard is the easiest way to oversee all your titles and view your sales reports. When you see your first sale, it will show up on your Dashboard. I check my sales at least once a day. It's so exciting to see those dollars add up!

I have one more secret for you. Let's say you submit your proof, everything is great, and your book gets listed on Amazon. A few months later, a buyer contacts you and says, "I thought your book was great, but you forgot to mention ___X___!" You're *mortified*. How could you forget to include something so important? But the book is already published! What can you do?

Well, here's the best part of POD publishing. You can make changes to your interior file even *after* you've submitted the book for publishing! Here's what you have to do to change your manuscript after the book has been submitted for publishing:

1. Make your desired changes, and create a brand new PDF file. Make very sure that your formatting still looks good. The last thing you want to do is introduce errors into the revised manuscript!

2. Go into your CreateSpace Dashboard and click on your book's title. At the top of the page, you will see this:

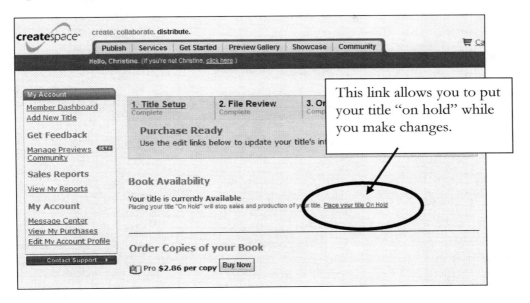

3. Use the link to put your title "on hold." This will allow you to make changes and upload a new interior file.

4. Upload a new interior file. You can only update the interior, not the cover. At the time of this printing, you could not make changes to the cover after you had submitted the book for publishing. Sorry.

5. You will need to submit your book for review again. CreateSpace employees will review the book for formatting problems, just like last time.

6. Once CreateSpace approves the interior file, just order a proof and make the title active again as soon as you get the proof. That's it!

I made changes to this title a few times as CreateSpace added new features and services. This way, you can always keep your book up to date. You are not really publishing a new edition. In traditional publishing, authors frequently make corrections to their books with subsequent "printings."

But what if you want to create a completely new edition? Well, you can. But you cannot re-use the same ISBN. If you do want to create a new edition of the book with a new cover, etc., you will have to submit a completely new title with a different ISBN number.

Chapter 7: Promoting Your Book on Amazon

"Forget bookstores.
Yes, I said it: Forget bookstores."

-**Aaron Shepard**, author of *Aiming at Amazon*

Promoting on Amazon

Promoting a book on Amazon is an art. Since you are publishing with CreateSpace, Amazon is going to be the main retailer for your book, unless you decide to print and sell copies of the book yourself (which most authors also do).

The best book on the market for this particular type of promotion is Aaron Shepard's *Aiming at Amazon*. Shepard is a master of online promotion, and his excellent book covers most of the tricks you need to know in order to promote your book on Amazon.

If you want to promote your book locally, consider purchasing Patricia Fry's superb book, *The Right Way to Write, Publish and Sell Your Book*. Fry has successfully published and marketed numerous regional books. I would also recommend Peter Bowerman's *The Well-Fed Self-Publisher*. Bowerman's book is funny, informative, and contains lots of great marketing information that will teach you how to self-publish profitably. Bowerman is not a fan of POD publishing, but his book is a marketing goldmine.

A number of basic, inexpensive marketing techniques will help you boost sales and get free publicity for your book. Whether you are painfully shy or a natural salesperson, you need to learn how to market your book. The more you learn about book marketing, the better.

Some authors find marketing themselves distasteful. Get over it. Buyers do not follow publishers. Buyers follow *authors*. So your first step in this marketing game is to get your name out there. Even authors who publish with traditional publishers must do a lot of their own marketing.

Amazon Profiles and Amazon's Author Central

Setting up your public persona is the next step in the book marketing game. Amazon allows you to have TWO profiles. You can have a public profile and an Author's Profile. The profiles are completely separate. The public profile is attached to your buyer's account. Anyone who buys books on Amazon has a public profile. Every time you post a book review, your public profile is available for everyone else to see.

An Author's Profile is only available to published authors. Once your book is published with CreateSpace and the listing is live on Amazon, you will be able to set up your Author's Profile. Let's cover your public profile first.

Setting up your public profile on Amazon

Your public profile already exists if you have ever purchased a book from Amazon or written a review for a book. You simply need to set it up. Just log into your Amazon account and pull up your information. Go to: **Your Account> Personalization>Your Public Profile>Edit Your Profile.** This is where you can update your public profile.

If you are already signed into your Amazon account, you can also visit your Amazon profile at:

www.amazon.com/gp/pdp/profile

You can upload a profile photograph and include a short biography. Update your display name. Your display name should be your pen name, even if you use a different name to purchase your items. If you have a professional designation, such as "CPA" or "Certified Personal Trainer," make sure you include that in your profile. Readers like to see that you are "an expert." You can change your display name at any time.

Amazon doesn't like authors to post websites in their book reviews, and Amazon makes it difficult for authors to make their personal websites part of their personal profile. Since Amazon will not allow links in your book reviews, you have to get imaginative. You can get around this by posting your website instead of your "location" in your profile. Nobody really needs to know where you live, anyway. It's better for potential buyers to see your website listed instead of where you reside.

When you write a book review for a book, your public profile will be updated automatically. Write book reviews for all the books you have in your personal library, especially if the books are on the same subject matter as the book you've written. This is a great way to boost your visibility on Amazon and get your name and website posted all over Amazon. It's free publicity and worth the effort.

Setting up an Author's Profile on Amazon

The second profile is your Author's Profile. The "Author Profile" is Amazon's program through *Author Central.* Author Central is a brand new service created just for authors. It is available only to published authors who have their books listed on Amazon. As soon as your book is listed on Amazon, you will be able to sign up for your Author's Page. If you have already published a book, even with a different publisher, you can sign up for an Author's Page.

Do it right away! Sign up at:

www.authorcentral.amazon.com

Your Author's Page will allow you to reach more readers, promote your books, and give your buyers a way to contact you through your website. You can also start an author's blog, or use the RSS feed from your existing blog.

Amazon allows you to upload a picture, a short bio, your contact information, and your website. Once you set up your profile in Author Central, buyers can see your public profile on Amazon whenever they click on your name. Buyers who look at your book listing on Amazon can click on the link under your name, and they will immediately be taken to your Author's Page.

Take the time to set up both of your Amazon profiles as quickly as possible. Cultivate them both and update them with new information often.

Chapter 8: Marketing Your Book Online

"As nonfiction publishers, our job is to crank out good, useful information that readers will buy and of a quality that they will come back for more. You need to finish the project and move on to another one if you want to make a living as a publisher. Success comes in numbers. The more products you have available, the more you will sell, and the more you will earn."

-Nick Russell, Publishing 4 Profit

Targeting Your Market

This is a good time to say a word about targeting your market. If you have experience in a particular industry, you want to focus your marketing efforts on those potential buyers. Realize that no two books are alike, but you will maximize your earning potential if you write about the same or similar subjects. After you get established, you can branch out into other industries or subjects. But at the beginning, you will have greater success if you focus your efforts in one direction.

The first book you publish will be your "anchor." This book introduces your nonfiction writing to the public, and it becomes the leader for any series, articles, or reports that you want to produce. Books naturally create extension products.

You can do speaking engagements, sell Internet goods, and promote derivative articles that are based on your book. This is called "compounding"—it's a process by which one book creates secondary products that also generate revenue. Once you write one book, you can re-adapt the information into derivative works that will make even more money. This is similar to the benefits of doing a series.

Many authors publish one book and then publish e-books, booklets, CDs, and DVDs based on the same material. You can do this and sell all of these derivative products on your website. Create a series of well-written books and other products that appeal to your existing audience and **you will succeed**.

The Right Niche Can Make You Rich

To make money as a self-publisher you have to find a niche market and "work it" thoroughly. It just makes more sense to research and publish a series of products aimed toward the same audience, rather than something on home improvement today, something else on fly fishing tomorrow, and something on skydiving next week.

With a series of products aimed toward one area of interest, you can focus your research and marketing to produce and sell products to the same audience over and over again, rather than starting from scratch with every project.

What is a niche market? Simply put, it is an area of interest that you are familiar with. With a good niche, you can develop written products for a wide enough audience to be profitable. By developing a series of products aimed at a niche market, you can sell them in different formats, and it becomes easy to develop an interested and willing audience who are ready to purchase other products you create.

What niche market works for you? The perfect niche market will have an audience of potential customers who need the specialized information you can offer them, and who have the money to pay for it. The larger the potential audience the better, but even small niches can be developed into profitable marketing opportunities.

Are you interested in classic cars? If so, you could produce booklets and books on restoring classic Mustangs, Thunderbirds, Corvettes, and GTOs. Much of the information will be applicable to any vintage automobile, but with research you can uncover restoration secrets that apply to specific models. How do you release that interior door panel on a 1969 Corvette without damaging it? How does one decipher the serial number code on an early Mustang to determine what drive train it came from the factory with? What options were available on which model years of early Firebirds?

By creating a series of booklets for different models of cars that includes both general restoration tips and model-specific information, you can appeal to owners of many different cars. You can also create a series of instructional DVDs for specific cars.

Maybe you love dogs. If so, you could develop a series of booklets on housebreaking puppies, grooming, solving behavioral problems, training service dogs, and showing dogs in competition. Again, you could tailor each booklet to a specific breed, or go with a general interest publication that covers all breeds.

One true-life example is an automotive technician who wrote a booklet on how to apply window tinting to car windows. The booklet was successful, so the author had his friends videotape him doing window-tinting jobs at his shop. He then sold the DVDs on his website for specific car models. He sells hundreds of these how-to DVDs every year. These are called derivative products, and they allow you to make "spin-off" revenue from your books.

Over time, you can take the wealth of information you have produced in your booklets and repackage it into a book, CD, DVD, newsletter, or series of special reports. You may decide to publish a monthly, bimonthly, or quarterly magazine or tabloid for your niche market, which will produce income from subscriptions and advertising revenue, and serve as a vehicle to market your future books and other products. You will certainly want to have a website dedicated to your niche market.

Anything and everything your potential niche audience wants to know is out there. You just have to do the research to find it for them. Once you produce and package your items, they will sell for years with proper marketing. Over time, you will become "the expert" in your niche, and your readers will seek you out, as well as suggest other products that they need and you can produce.

So find your niche, explore it, and learn what information your potential customers need, and then fill that need! [P]

It's Easier to Fish in the Same Pond!

Having a specific niche also will help you when it comes to marketing your book. One of the basic rules of marketing is that it's always easier to market to existing customers rather than trying to go out and snag new ones. If you focus on one subject, you will cultivate readers that will become your fans and will purchase everything you write. Your income will compound when you have more books in the market on similar subjects. The most successful nonfiction writers use compounding techniques in order to maximize their earning potential.

They start with a first book, add on a newsletter, publish an e-book, and publish a second book, and so on—all on the same subject matter. It's so easy to market to your existing customers. Build up an e-mail list. Encourage posts on your blog. Include an advertisement in all of your books for your other writing. Create a simple catalog and upload it to your website. Have a little picture of your book/booklet, along with a short description, and an order form so people can order directly from you if they want. Your first book is your anchor. Everything else you create can spin off from it.

Create Derivative Products

Each book creates multiple opportunities to generate revenue on derivatives. The next book can continue on in a similar (but unique) subject, which then generates even more derivative products. Example: do you love breeding Labrador Retrievers? Write a series of books about Labradors—breeding them, showing them, and training them. Each book promotes the next. Once you have your first book written, you can create derivative products such as:

- **Articles:** You can market your articles online and to magazines. Make sure that you include a byline that tracks back to your website and your book. Even if the articles don't generate any direct income, they will generate free publicity.
- **Newsletters:** Online newsletters are a great way to advertise your books, products, and services. Once you have an e-mail list, you can send out monthly or weekly newsletters on various topics related to your books. Once again, the material all helps promote your books.

- **Special Reports:** Many writers sell special reports. Dan Poynter, Nick Russell, and Dale Beaumont are writers who all have made money selling special reports. These are essentially smaller condensed chapters, or updated information that would be helpful to your existing readers. Most authors sell their special reports through their websites.
- **Seminars and Webinars:** Don't be shy! You can also make money selling your information in person. Seminars are a big money-maker for authors. You can offer speaking engagements for a fixed fee, and then generate additional revenue by selling your books, CDs, and reports at the event. Instead of book signings, consider free "seminars," which will draw larger crowds and still be profitable.
- **Audiobooks and CDs:** Busy people love audiobooks and CDs. They can listen to them while driving and doing other tasks, like cleaning the house. You already have the material—why not transform it into an audiobook?

Marketing at Special Events

Many authors use special events to market their books. If you enjoy marketing in person and meeting your fans, this is a great way to get exposure for your book. Some authors are natural salespeople. If you have a gift for sales and have an outgoing personality, you will do well with in-person marketing techniques.

Book Signings

A book signing is not the best way to market a book, but many authors enjoy doing them. Book signings are **most** profitable when they are **combined** with another activity. And book signings don't have to happen at bookstores. If you write a book about quilting, consider a seminar/book signing at your local craft store. If you write a book about sport fishing, consider a book signing and a reading at a local fishing club or marina. The opportunities are endless if you are creative and persistent! If you are nervous in front of groups, consider taking a speech class or joining Toastmasters.

Book Fairs

Book fairs can also be a great venue to promote your book. Talk to other authors (but don't be rude about it—they are trying to sell their products too!) See how other writers promote their books. Some will be successful, and others will not. If you belong to any professional organizations, they will send newsletters announcing upcoming book fairs. At first, you can attend the book fairs as a participant. Have fun, and talk to other authors and see how everyone is promoting their books. Later, you can purchase a booth, or, even better, join up with another author and co-sponsor a booth together. This is the time to make relationships that will be beneficial to your future marketing efforts.

Book Reviews

It's your job to contact the people who will review your book and possibly promote it. You must invest in book reviews in order to be successful (more on this later). For example, Nick Russell, founder of the *Gypsy Journal*, regularly hands out free copies of his newspaper at every new RV campground he visits. He also hands out free copies at RV rallies and trade shows. He gets dozens of "residual" subscriptions from this promotional activity.

**Nick Russell on
Face-to-Face Promotion**

We always hand out free copies of the *Gypsy Journal* at RV trade shows, and I carry copies with us at all times. At a new RV park, we will leave copies for other RVers to read. This generates a steady stream of subscribers—not right away, but people take the newspaper home and read it, and then subscribe. Sometimes even weeks later, the subscriptions come trickling in, three or four at a time. The cost is negligible to us, and the free copies always generate referrals. Of course, the newspaper is our flagship product, and the books, special reports, and CDs sell once people get signed up for the newspaper.

Join Local Networking Organizations

Business connections are especially beneficial. Make sure you have quality stationery, business cards, and brochures when you attend events. Be visible in community business-related affairs (charity balls, cook-outs, fundraisers).

Join your local Chamber of Commerce and attend as many functions as you can. This is especially true if you write exclusively for a specific industry. If you write books about horses, go to riding events and horse shows. Communicate and get your name out there. If you write books about accounting, join accounting organizations and attend continuing education events. Talk to people. If you're a travel writer, attend seminars and events for travel agents and other travel writers. Get the picture?

If you have any connections to a certain industry through past business dealings or friends and acquaintances, now is the time to let them know that you have written a book of interest to them. Networking is an incredibly powerful way to find new buyers "out of the blue."

Pass around your business cards. Dress professionally (no sneakers, no jeans, no mini-skirts, no torn clothing). If you're shy or don't like public gatherings, you can still have a strong online presence. Join newsgroups, post a blog every day, or create an e-mail newsletter. Use online forums to promote your website, book, and writing. Get your name and your book out there any way you can!

CreateSpace Marketing Services

CreateSpace, in conjunction with BookSurge, has recently decided to start offering book marketing services. For a fee, CreateSpace will compose a press release, a publicity kit, postcards, sell sheets—you name it! They will create all types of printed material for you to submit to reviewers, radio stations, etc. Your book must already be listed for sale in order to take advantage of the CreateSpace marketing program.

Unfortunately, you cannot order marketing services until after your book has been submitted for final publication. I think that this is a detriment to authors, because many authors want professional advice on how to compose their promotional copy for the back of the book, but CreateSpace's position on the matter is unlikely to change.

CreateSpace offers a press release with distribution, which sends information about your book to media outlets. The press release service starts at $199 and goes up from there. There is no guarantee of additional sales, so if you are on a tight budget, you may want to forgo the added marketing costs. However, if you have the extra money, or if this is your first book, you may want to try promoting the book using CreateSpace marketing services. Do NOT invest money in marketing services at the expense of giving up a good copy editor. Editing is more important than even marketing—if your book is poorly written, your marketing efforts will only backfire as readers begin to write negative reviews of your book.

The CreateSpace marketing services seem professional enough, but if you are on a limited budget, you may want to pass on these pricey extras and do the majority of your own marketing.

CreateSpace Publishing Services

As of late 2009, CreateSpace has started to offer complete publishing packages, which include custom cover design, formatting, and ISBN assignment. The packages start at $758 and go up to $4,346. The more expensive packages include editing. CreateSpace now also offers basic copyediting services starting at $190 for 10,000 words.

I would recommend using these services only if you *really* have the money to spend. I use my own freelance editor, and you can too. If money is no object, but you have had difficulty getting accepted by a traditional publisher, then by all means, purchase these author's services.

However, if you are on a tight budget, I really recommend that you try to learn how to format the book yourself. Learn how to use the Cover Creator and experiment using different cover art or photographs. You can also look through the author's services and order many of them a la carte. Whatever you do, don't forgo the use of a copyeditor in order to purchase advertising.

Make sure your book is the highest possible quality in terms of content, grammar, and punctuation. Then, (and only if you have money left over) invest the rest of your budget in advertising and other add-ons.

Chapter 9: Promote with Book Reviews

"Book reviews **sell books**...A book review is an excellent way to promote your book for free. There are countless opportunities out there for getting your book reviewed. It's just a matter of finding the right place."

-Patricia Fry, author of
The Right Way to Write, Publish, and Sell Your Book

Sending Out Review Copies

Many writers believe that book reviews are the most cost-effective way to promote a book. When you publish with CreateSpace, you will be able to purchase books very cheaply. You can send copies to reviewers in order to get free publicity for your book. You MUST invest in book reviews in order to be successful. Reviews are free advertising, and they are better than paid advertising because readers are more inclined to believe a reviewer than a regular paid ad.

Find your target audience. Contact as many websites, forums, newsgroups, and associations as you can via e-mail or by phone. Ask if you can send them a complimentary review copy of your book. Don't send out unsolicited copies, however. Make sure you contact someone and get a name and an address.

All successful self-published authors use book reviews, to some extent, in their marketing programs. A professional review promotes your book for free, and it adds legitimacy to your work. An editorial is always better than a printed advertisement. It's the cheapest way to promote your book without having to pay for print advertising.

Print advertising and direct mail are the **worst** ways to promote your book. Both are expensive and produce a poor return. However, if you send out a review copy and get your book featured in a magazine or editorial, your only cost is the wholesale cost of the book and the postage. No advertising costs, and readers are more likely to read your book review rather than an advertisement. What a bargain!

Once you publish your book and it becomes available on Amazon, your readers will be able to post Amazon reviews. Not all your reviews will be positive, but studies have shown that even negative reviews add credibility to a book. So if you do receive a negative review, don't be discouraged. Take the information under advisement. Negative reviews can make you a better writer.

There are many ways to get book reviews. First, make sure all your friends and professional connections have a copy of the book. Ask them to post their honest opinion on Amazon. You should contact as many organizations that are related to your book as possible. Don't just send them the book. CALL THEM. Get the name of a manager or someone who actually has some decision-making power. Ask if you can send them a copy of your book for "professional review." It makes people feel important. The smaller the organization, the better luck you will have with honest feedback.

HINT: People get really impressed when they are talking to authors. It doesn't matter if you are publishing out of a trailer park somewhere—if you start your call with, "Yes, this is David Smith. I am the author of *Gorgeous Gladiolas,* and I was hoping to speak with Fannie Jones, the head of the Western Gardening Club. I am eager to send Ms. Jones a complimentary copy of my book in order to get her opinion."

That's it! You're almost guaranteed to get a response. When you send out your book, include a nice letter and some promotional material for the book, such as a press release or a descriptive flier (which you can craft yourself or purchase from CreateSpace's new marketing services program). Book testimonials, especially when posted on Amazon, stimulate interest in your book. Kindly request that your reviewer post a testimonial on your Amazon item detail page.

Ask to use the testimonials on your website too. Positive testimonials and book reviews from friends and colleagues are free. Make sure you have the budget for at least 25-100 review copies.

Before sending them out, make sure that all of your review copies are stamped with a **"Review Copy"** stamp. You can custom-order a stamp online for about $15. Although authors have no legal standing to prevent a review copy from being re-sold, stamping the book prevents most re-selling abuse. Amazon's official policy prohibits the sale of review copies.

Promotional versions of all media, including books (advance reading copies and uncorrected proofs), music, and videos are prohibited. These items are distributed for promotional consideration and are not authorized for retail sale.

-Amazon Policy on Promotional Books

This is difficult to police because Amazon can't possibly monitor millions of booksellers at once. Students, scammers, and non-legitimate reviewers may all try to scam a free copy of the book from you. These copies are often re-sold to used bookstores or online. It happens, and even if you stamp your book, there's a chance that the book will still be re-sold.

How to Prepare Your Review Request

After you've gathered the contact information for a potential reviewer, you have to prepare the testimonial sheet. It's also a good idea to include a release form so that you have permission to use the review and the reviewer's name.

Reviews are essential to your success. There's also a good chance that you will get valuable feedback on how to improve your book.

You should request an endorsement from **at least** ten peers: colleagues, friends, and acquaintances in the same profession. Contact these people in advance to let them know you are sending a copy of your book along with a review request. When you send out books for review, always include a clearly printed, one-page sheet with the following information:

- Title
- Your name (or pen name)
- Publisher's name, address, and contact person (if you are a one-person show, this is a good time to consider using a pen name because it makes your "organization" look larger)
- Address, telephone number, e-mail address
- Publication date
- Price and ordering information, including name of distributors (CreateSpace)
- A brief summary of the book
- A short author's bio (three to four lines maximum)

If you aren't sure about the reviewer's sex, ***don't guess!*** Just use their entire name (Dear Pat Smith).

You don't have to be shy or embarrassed to ask for a review or a testimonial.

When you ask for the review, just be professional and friendly. Often, the providers of testimonials are flattered by the request. When published authors talk, people listen!

If you are confident enough, you should consider soliciting an endorsement from other professional authors or leaders in your field. Contact information is easily obtained online. Usually, all you have to do is a little digging in order to get the contact information for the people you want to review your book. The worst they can say is "no," so give it a try.

Here's an example of a review request letter:

Sample Review Request Letter

Pat A. Cox
Editor-in-Chief
Midwest Book Review
278 Orchard Drive
Oregon, WI 53575-1129

Dear Pat Cox,
I'm the author of *True Crime Bloodhound Stories*, a book that I hope you will consider for review.

This book is a collection of real-life bloodhound stories from police officers across the country. The bloodhound is famous for its ability to follow scents hours or even days old and over great distances. The book details true accounts of criminals captured by this amazing breed.

I have enclosed a review copy. *True Crime Bloodhound Stories* is published by Brandywine Small Press (Sacramento, CA, January 2010) and retails for $15.99. I've included a few recent book reviews as well as a brief bio.

Thank you for your consideration.

Best Regards,
Bill Barnes
Brandywine Small Press
12345 Main Street
Sacramento CA 95823
916-123-4567
BillBarnes@BrandywinePR.com

Here's an example of a testimonial permission form:

Testimonial Permission Form

By completing this form, you are allowing Brandywine Small Press to reprint all or a portion of your comments online or in print. We will not publish full names, phone numbers, or e-mail addresses. Please sign the completed form and return it by (specify a date). Please keep the enclosed review copy of the book for your reading enjoyment.

Name: _____ Phone: _____

Company: _____ Website: _____

Address: _____

City: _____ State: _____ Zip: _____

Testimonial: _____
_____
_____
_____

Signature _____

Thank you for taking the time to fill out this testimonial. We value your comments and we may include them in one of our future books, articles, or on our website.

As you receive more testimonials, add them to your website or your testimonial sheet. As you collect more testimonials, replace older testimonials with newer ones you prefer. Dan Poynter has a good special report on his website on how to obtain testimonials. Visit *www.parapublishing.com* to obtain his special report called *"Blurbs for Your Books: Testimonials, Endorsements and Quotations."*

There are also many resources online that will give you information on how to get an honest and useful book review.

The Midwest Book Review

A great resource is the Midwest Book Review, established in 1976 (***www.midwestbookreview.com***). This website has excellent resources on how to get reviewed, who to contact, and even how to become a professional reviewer yourself! The Midwest Book Review also has a posted list of book review magazines that are used by librarians. There is also a long list of reviewers that you can use as a reference. The Midwest Book Review has a great reputation and does not accept money for reviews.

Go to the Midwest Review website and read the articles posted there. The information is highly useful to any author who is looking for professional reviews.

List of Book Reviewers

I maintain a list of free (non-fee based) book reviewers on my website, *www.stepbystepselfpublishing.net.* All of the book reviewers accept self-published books.

It's a great resource for new authors or anyone who just doesn't know where to start looking for book publicity. You can see the reviewer's preferred genre (some accept fantasy, romance, children's books, etc.) Contact the reviewer first by e-mail before sending your book. If they accept your submission, make sure you include a letter with all your contact information and information about your book. Give the reviewer at least a month to review the book. It is okay to send an e-mail to make sure that the book was received if you haven't heard anything in four to six weeks.

All the reviewers that I contacted were gracious and polite, and once I accumulated a nice bunch of reviews, I updated my manuscript to include some positive quotes from the reviews at the front of this book (see pages 1-2).

Investing In Book Reviews: by Nick Russell

Besides being a self-published author, I (Nick) am also the publisher of a nationally-circulated RV newspaper, the *Gypsy Journal.* In the past I owned several community newspapers. Over the years, I have reviewed hundreds of books. Unfortunately, there were many other good books that I never reviewed. Was this because of time constraints or a lack of space in my publications? Because they did not meet our editorial profile? No, the reason these books did not get a review is because their authors and/or publishers wanted me to **purchase** a copy for review!

They were not willing to provide even a copy of their book to get a review; they expected me to make the investment! How many potential buyers never heard about that book, because the author was too cheap to supply a review copy?

For any business to succeed, it must advertise. Review copies are the best advertising you can do. To sell a book, you must get it out there in front of readers. Book reviews do that for you. Yet I have talked to many authors over the years who just don't seem to understand that most publications aren't going to give them the time of day, much less any review space, if they are expected to purchase the book to do so!

Why should I, as a newspaper editor, be forced to buy your book to give **you** free publicity? What's in it for me? I'm not going to spend **my** money to give **you** free advertising. I already have plenty of material to fill my pages.

Recently I was strolling through the vendor area at an RV rally when I came across a booth where an author was displaying his book on RV travel. I picked up a copy, thumbed through it, and was impressed. The writing style seemed good, the layout and design were attractive, and the cover was eye-catching.

I introduced myself, gave him my business card and a copy of the *Gypsy Journal*, and complimented him on his book. We chatted for a few minutes, and then I offered to review his book in our next issue if he wanted to supply me with a review copy.

"Really?" he asked. "I've sent out eight or ten e-mails about my book and none of the other RV magazines has even replied! What's the secret to getting books reviewed?"

"Most won't respond to an e-mail," I told him. "I get dozens of e-mails every day. If you want a publication to review your book, you have to find out who handles the reviews, and send him or her a letter introducing your book and offering to supply a review copy. Or better yet, send them a letter and a copy of the book up front. They may not have the time to respond to your letter, but if they have the book in front of them to look at, your chances of getting it reviewed are much better."

"Then how do I get paid? Do I just send them an invoice for the book with the cover letter?" he asked.

"You don't get paid," I told him, "It's a review copy. The magazine is doing you a favor by reviewing your book so their readers will know about it and want to buy it."

"So they don't pay me for the book?" he asked incredulously. "They expect me to give it to them? How can I make any money that way?"

"You don't make any money off that particular copy of the book," I tried to explain. "Think of a review copy as advertising. You make money off the sale of all of the other books that the review will hopefully generate."

"Yeah, hopefully," he said, "and if nobody buys anything from the review, I'm out the cost of a book! What a racket! If anybody wants to review my book, they'll pay for it just like everyone else!"

I handed him his book back, wished him well, and walked away.

I'd like to think that this was an isolated case of a self-publisher who just had not done his homework and does not understand how this business works. Unfortunately, that is not the case. Over the years I have had many authors and publishers solicit me for a review, and then expect me to purchase their book so I can review it.

When I read for pleasure, or to further my knowledge of a subject, I expect to pay for my books. But as a reviewer, I will invest my time in a suitable book for review, but not my money.

Chapter 10: Promoting Your Book on the Internet

"Marketing your book is a matter of making friends, lots of friends."

-**John Kremer**, Founder of **BookMarket**

Get a Website—Now!

In the twenty-first century, having a website is a necessity. Your website serves as your online brochure. It works for you twenty-four hours a day, and is always there when a potential reader wants to find information about who you are and what your small press has to offer.

Studies show that buyers rarely look up a publisher's website, but they will often research an author before they buy a book. See if your pen name is available as a domain right now. Try different variations if your name is a common one. For example, if your pen name is Lorraine Davenport, try the following:

www.LorraineDavenport.com
www.LDavenport.com
www.LoriDavenport.com
www.LorrieDavenport.com
www.LDavenportWriter.com

You get the picture. Most authors will start out with a simple personal website, and graduate to a publishing site from there. I currently have four websites and two blogs (and counting!). A website is one of the cheapest and most efficient forms of advertising for your books.

I recommend that you purchase a domain and a website right away. This may also be a big part of choosing your company name. Maybe you want to name your company "Davenport Small Press," but you find out that the domain, ***www.DavenportSmallPress.com*** (website address), is already taken. Someone is already using the perfect name that YOU picked out! The nerve!

So you have to choose another name. In doing a domain name search, you find out that ***www.DavenportBooks.com*** is available. Perfect. You purchase the domain and you're on your way. A side note: if you can't get a website address (domain name) ending in ".com" or ".net," then move on and think of something else. All the other domain addresses, such as ".info" or ".biz," are not suitable if you are trying to maximize your Internet search potential.

If you don't have a website for your writing, get one. Pronto! This can be done inexpensively and will open possibilities for promoting your writing and books without geographical restraints. Creating a website is easy. If you use a pre-designed template, you can do it yourself in just a few hours. Many hosting companies have simple website software that works online, and even use "drag-

and-drop" editing. We will go over some of these "simple website" providers in a moment. So stop making excuses. Get a website right away.

Your website will work best for you if it is simple. Your home page should be like a company brochure. It should be attractive and NOT about your personal life. Your website should instead focus on your qualifications, writing background, and published work. If you haven't published anything yet, you can focus on the book you are working on. Your contact information should be easy to find. Include links to more specific information about your services and credibility. You can choose to post a phone number or not. That's it! Keep it simple.

The purpose of your website is to get prospective buyers to see your writing and understand more about your company. Here are some other pointers:

- **Submit your website to search engines** – This takes a little time, but is worth it in the long run. While you're searching for local directories on the web, you might as well submit your website to the search engines. Eventually your URL (website address) will be added to their listings anyway, but that can take many months before it happens. You'll speed up the process a bit if you submit your URL directly.

- **Give testimonials and exchange links**– Do you work with another author or business that you like? Why not approach him or her and offer to provide a testimonial? Ask that your full name and company name be listed, along with a link to your website. That's a true win-win situation since your service provider gets the testimonial and you get a free link to your website. The networking website LinkedIn (**www.linkedin.com**) uses this theory. LinkedIn encourages its members to recommend other members—so everyone is "linked" by another business connection. Every little link helps.

It's also a great way to promote future projects. If you do have an e-mail newsletter, this is a great place for your readers to be able to opt-in and get a taste of what you have to offer.

Inexpensive (and Free) Web Hosting Services

I personally use **Microsoft Live Small Business** website service. It's reliable, free to set up, and if you purchase a custom domain, it only costs about $25 per year. I edit the site myself. The online page editing software is really easy to use, (and if you have HTML editing skills, you can do even fancier stuff.) Microsoft gives you everything you need to take your business online: free website hosting, free templates, and e-mail support. You can set up a PayPal shopping cart and market your book right from your website, if you want. I've even called Microsoft's phone support (they don't make it easy to find the number), and the operator was very courteous and professional, and stayed on the line with me until the problem was solved.

Where else can you get this much for $25 a year? You can find out more at:

http://www.officelive.com/free-website

The other free website provider I like is Weebly at ***www.weebly.com***. It's free to create a website, if you want to use a sub-domain through Weebly. After you decide on your company name and/or your pen name, you can purchase a custom domain in about five minutes.

A custom domain through Weebly costs about $55 a year, and this includes e-mail and web hosting. It's so simple that no one else can really hold a candle to their ease-of-use.

Weebly's drag-and-drop interface is extremely simple to use, and they also offer free web hosting. You can set up a website in less than an hour with Weebly, but it won't have some of the extra fancy features that the Microsoft Small Business service offers. So if you want super-easy, go with Weebly. If you want fancier extras, go with Microsoft.

If you sign up with Weebly, you can pay $3.99 per month to upgrade to Weebly PRO. This will allow you to remove all the ads off of your website. The additional $3.99 fee also allows you to get faster support—Weebly PRO customers always get put at the top of the e-mail queue. It's so cheap, and it's worth it! When you upgrade to Weebly Pro, you can create up to ten websites. I use Weebly to create websites highlighting my individual books.

GoDaddy also has an inexpensive service called "Website Tonight." It's about the same cost as Weebly and it's relatively easy to use. ***www.GoDadddy.com.***

If you don't have any money for a domain, all is not lost. There are many social networking sites where, once you join, you are provided a profile page. You can use that as your temporary website if necessary.

Here are a few free social networking sites to consider:

- **www.LinkedIn.com:** A popular social networking site, more designed for working professionals.
- **www.MySpace.com:** One of the first social networking sites.
- **www.Facebook.com:** Another popular social networking site.

Social networking sites are a good place to start, but you need to make sure that you eventually have a nice website for yourself and your books. It will cost you less than $50 to do it right, so don't skimp on getting a website. It's almost impossible to self-publish without one.

Get a Professional-Sounding E-Mail Address

When choosing your e-mail address, choose a good e-mail for your business based on your name or business name. Do NOT use a "funny" or "cute" e-mail address. This looks ridiculous to a potential client and may cause a client to disregard your services altogether. It goes without saying that if your e-mail address contains anything "sexual," either overtly or not, it is totally inappropriate to use for your business. Here are some amusing examples:

SexyGirl@mail.com
FunnyDude@mail.com
Chickenhead@mail.com
VampireLord@mail.com
GoodGuyGoneBad@us.com
JediMaster26@aol.com

None of these e-mail addresses is appropriate for a professional writer, business, or anything else other than communication with family and friends. You can get a free e-mail account from Yahoo in just a few minutes. Take the time to get a professional e-mail right away.

Start a Company E-Newsletter

An e-mail newsletter is one of the most effective yet inexpensive marketing tools available. As long as you have a valid e-mail address for your readers or industry contacts, you can send them a newsletter. If you already have an existing relationship, it is a great way to keep in touch with your existing readers. You can purchase an easy template online and make your newsletter look professional.

An e-mail newsletter is an excellent marketing tool and serves an educational function as well as a contact method. A newsletter sent electronically costs you nothing, and it gives you the opportunity to highlight your knowledge and skills to your readers and other potential buyers. You must, however, have people subscribe to your newsletter if you will distribute it via e-mail.

A monthly newsletter takes a few hours of work, but the rewards can be enormous. If done correctly, it can build your reputation and prestige, and the resulting word-of-mouth referrals will more than make up for your time spent.

Of course, if you have an existing list of readers, send the newsletter to them, and ask if they can forward it to any friends or family who might be interested in your book.

IMPORTANT: You should use an e-mail service to manage your e-mail marketing. There are laws against sending unsolicited e-mail of a marketing nature. DO NOT attempt to send your newsletters from your own e-mail account, such as through Outlook.

Not only will you have difficulties when your list grows to more than about fifty addresses, you will also run into problems with your e-mail provider. Unsolicited e-mail of a marketing nature is known as SPAM and it is against the law!

You will need to subscribe to a newsletter and e-mail management service such as *Aweber* (**www.aweber.com**). These services are inexpensive (starting at about $15 per month) and will help manage your mailing list. Anyone who subscribes to your list will use what is called an *opt-in* system. This means that they have given you permission to send them e-mail about your book.

These e-mail marketing services will also help you to make sure that your newsletter has an attractive look. The content of your newsletter should be geared toward your target audience and include information that is helpful to the readers; otherwise, they will unsubscribe from your newsletter.

For example, if you specialize in books for beauty shops, make sure that your newsletter includes good tips geared toward beauty shop owners. Make your newsletters educational and informative. The newsletter should not be filled with solicitation. Potential clients dislike an overload of sales type messages, as do we all.

Easy "Soft-Sell" Promotion Tactics

Having a website or a profile on the web will not help you if no one sees it. If you build it, but no one knows it exists, potential buyers won't know about your book. And you don't want just any traffic either. You want readers who are looking for your book so that you can generate sales fast.

You can accomplish this quickly and with little or no cost. Here are some small ways you can start to get traffic on its way to your website. No one method will bring you a stampede of traffic. But using these techniques on a consistent basis will pay off in the long run.

- **E-mail Signature**: Create a signature file that will list your company name and contact information, as well as any benefit-driven catch phrase that will draw everyone who reads your e-mails to learn more about your books and what you have to offer. Be sure to include an **active link** to your website. Every time you send out an e-mail, your e-signature is attached. That means, at least potentially, everyone who gets your e-mail can drive more traffic to your website. It's a wonderful soft-sell tactic that works.

- **Online Message Signature**: Using the same principle as an e-mail signature, include with your name a link to your website in any and all posts you may make to online blogs or message forums. You never know who might be reading your comments and just might have a burning need for your books.

- **List Your Website in Free Online Directories**: Local directories are the phone books of today. Most of the popular Internet search engines have them. As of the writing of this book, both Google and Yahoo offer free listings in their local directories.

Compounding Your Profits

Remember that the more you write and promote your area of expertise, the better the chance that you will be able to support yourself entirely off your writing. One nonfiction book is difficult to market—but multiple books, a newsletter, and a few special reports (all on the same subject) are a goldmine!

Compounding your profits is a very simple idea based upon maximizing the amount of financial return you receive for the time, money, and energy invested in your work.

You shouldn't just write something and sell it. You create a concept that you can sell, repackage in another format, and sell again to the same buyers or to an entirely new audience, then repackage and sell it again, and then again! You should be able to write it once and market or use it at least four times in different formats. Some of those formats include, but are not limited to:

1. Books
2. Articles
3. Booklets
4. e-books
5. Audio books on CD
6. Instructional DVDs
7. Seminars and speaking engagements
8. Special reports

The idea is to create an interlocking inventory of written work that you can market over and over again. The additional products you write and publish will promote the sale of subsequent articles, books, etc.

Instead of writing something, selling it, and moving on to something completely new, you can create an ongoing stream of revenue. Instead of having to come up with new projects all of the time, by creating a series of products that can be used over and over again and that help sell other products, you can get the very best return for the time you have invested in creating the item originally, and you can spend more of your time marketing and bringing in money. [9]

All of your books should at the very least contain:

- A listing of your other books, e-books, or DVDs
- An advertising page for your website, newsletter, or blog
- Internal references to your other books, articles, etc.
- An author bio listing your personal website, accomplishments, and the best way to contact your company

The Gypsy Journal RV Newspaper

www.gypsyjournal.net
Case Study of Success

Nick Russell is the publisher of the *Gypsy Journal*. It's a bi-monthly, thirty-six page tabloid newspaper for RVers, a highly targeted, niche market. Each issue includes stories about places for RVers to visit, articles on the RV lifestyle, and columns of interest to RVers.

Nick's primary niche market is recreational vehicle travelers. He serves them with the *Gypsy Journal* RV Travel Newspaper, www.gypsyjournal.net, with five books, (all written for the RV crowd), eight booklets, and several CDs. Nick also presents RV lifestyle seminars at RV rallies and shows. He writes about the lifestyle he loves, and his writing allows him to travel and RV full-time.

One popular feature of the *Gypsy Journal* is a travelogue in every issue titled **Meandering Down the Highway**. In each issue, this piece runs from 7,000 to 10,000 words. Nick compiled the first year's worth of **Meandering Down the Highway** columns into a self-published book by the same name, resulting in a new product to sell to readers. From that book, Nick created a seminar by the same name that he presents at RV shows and at the "Life on Wheels" RV conferences.

He also publishes an abbreviated version of the **Meandering Down the Highway** column on his website at **www.gypsyjournal.net**. He allows a couple of newspapers to publish excerpts from the **Meandering Down the Highway** column in their pages, with a byline and reference to his website, driving more traffic and sales toward the website. He writes the column once and re-formats and re-uses it at least four times. That really beats having to create something new all of the time! Nick sells books through:

1. Advertisements in the *Gypsy Journal*
2. His website
3. Other RV-related websites on a commission basis
4. RV shows and rallies

At conventions, Nick books speaking engagements or vendor booths. At his vendor booths and seminars, his books are always neatly displayed. The inside cover of each book lists all of his books, booklets, and other products for sale. All the booklets also list his products.

He created one product (a book), and he uses the same information in columns in the newspaper, on his website, and at every RV show he attends. In addition, the product listing on the inside back covers of the booklets brings in even more sales! Everything works together to create and increase his income stream. This is called *cross-promotion*.

Blogging for Dollars

Through the *Gypsy Journal*, Nick has built a loyal following of people eager to buy his books and other products. You can also build a loyal audience through blogging, and get paid to do so.

A blog is a type of online diary and is one of the easiest ways to promote your books and make additional revenue. Now, this shouldn't be an actual diary. Don't post information about your personal life. A short author's bio is sufficient. Nobody really wants to know that you have seven cats and a parakeet named Stinky. The more professional-looking your blog, the more earning potential you will have. Use the blog as a springboard to promote everything you write—your books, your articles, your website—everything! And add your blog and your website to your e-mail signature, so every e-mail that you send out to anyone, anywhere, creates a potential source of referrals and ad revenue.

You can use a blog as your website, although you should eventually have a professional website apart from your blog. The easiest blog website is **www.blogger.com**, although there are dozens of other providers with free blog hosting, and you can research which one you like the best.

Blogger is a simple and quick way to get a blog up and running. You can use it as a professional diary, to run a blog for your company, or to promote your writing to potential readers or publishers. Blogger is now owned by Google and is ranked sixteenth in the world in terms of website popularity. Best of all, it's still free.

At the beginning, it may seem that you're too busy to write a weekly blog. You might have multiple writing projects, and working on a blog just seems like extra work. Well, that's a crock! A blog is an invaluable marketing tool—most blogging services are free, and it only takes about thirty minutes a week to compose a blog post. Change your thinking—a blog can ALSO be a great source of passive revenue.

While researching some information for one of my publishing seminars, I came across several references to blogging and followed a link or two, and realized that there is an entire income stream out there I had been overlooking!

Google, the online search engine, provides an advertising program called **Google AdSense** that puts money in online publishers' pockets every month. In some cases, it's BIG money!

The process is simple. After registering with Google AdSense, bloggers can quickly and easily paste a simple HTML code into their web pages. Once they publish or update their blog or website, Google's webcrawlers search the web pages and insert small ad links leading to advertisers with products or services relevant to the web page or blog content. Whenever one of your website's visitors clicks on a Google ad link on your site, you receive a small commission.

The more pages and content you add to your websites and blog, the more your AdSense commissions go up. Different ad links produce different commissions, and they can range from a few cents for some of the ads to $2 or more for ad links on the publishing website.

Now, don't get greedy and start clicking on your own ad links, or have all of your friends get online clicking the ad links! Google calls that "click fraud" and will quickly slap you down for that.

Recourse for click fraud can be as simple as a stern warning letter, or it may cause you to lose hundreds of dollars in ad commissions, or even to have your Google AdSense account canceled. So just play the game right, and, as with any business project, let it grow over time.

For more information on the AdSense program, or to sign up, go to:

www.google.com/adsense

Some people blog full-time and actually earn a nice living doing so. Blogging full-time is real work, and it can take years to build a full-time income, but it is possible. The idea is to create blogs that people "follow" every single day. Once your blog generates enough web traffic, the advertising on the blogs generates revenues.

According to ProBlogger, about half of the bloggers surveyed made little or no money through blogging, and the rest of the people surveyed made varying amounts.[ ] A smaller percentage, about 30 percent, made a few hundred dollars a month. Nick Russell reported to me that his blog generates anywhere from $400 to $600 per month. So it's reasonable to assume that you can make money blogging too. If you work hard at your blog and it generates nice traffic, you could be earning at least a few hundred dollars per month in ad-click revenues.

And blogging is something that will promote all your other writing, so it's really a win-win situation.

You can post links on your blog to numerous revenue-generating websites, and affiliate links from Amazon that go right to your book!

The Gypsy Journal
Blogging 4 Bucks!
Nick Russell

Publishing a daily blog has also brought in some other income as well. When I announced a year-end closeout on several of my RV books in the blog, a dozen or so orders came in within twenty-four hours. The blog also brought several paid reservations for an RV rally we had in February 2008, and when I announced the dates for the 2009 rally in the blog, several more paid reservations quickly arrived in response.

Following the Publishing 4 Profit methodology, I have been revising and using these daily blog entries as content for my *Meandering Down the Highway* column in our *Gypsy Journal* RV newspaper.

Our best single day of AdSense commissions has been just over $60, and we've had a couple of days where commissions were only a buck or two. On average we are earning around $20 to $23 a day at this point in commissions.

I (Christy, the author) have two blogs. The first blog is a book review website. It focuses mostly on publishing, marketing, promotion, and other topics that are important to freelance writers and self-published authors. This is "The Publishing Maven" at *www.selfpublishingreview.blogspot.com*. My second blog is my official author's blog at *www.christypinheiro.blogspot.com*.

My blogs promote my books and publishing efforts. All of the blogs are free on Blogger so my only expense is my time. Your blogs should do the same. Instead of spending your precious time writing about your dog Sparky and your trip to the Grand Canyon, set up a real writer's blog and start promoting your books. Blog about your niche. Blog about your publishing journey. Blog about your next project. And make sure that you have pictures and links to all your books so people know that you mean business. Soon, you will start generating comments, followers, and ad-click revenue. Promote, Promote, Promote.

Advertising Income

Many authors sell back-of-the-book advertising within their books. This is also called "in-book" advertising. You can sell the last few pages to an advertiser and earn money for those pages. For example, if your book is on quilt making, you may want to approach a local craft or fabric store and ask if they would like to advertise in your book. Tell them that they would get an exclusive ad, and you will offer copies of your book on consignment to them. It's a win-win situation for both of you!

Be careful, though. If you want to sell to bookstores, some bookstores won't carry books that include obvious print advertising. You have to weigh the benefits and risks of accepting advertising. For example, if you earn enough from print ads to pay for an entire print run of 1,000 books, it might be worth it for you to accept the advertising dollars and promote your book more aggressively to non-bookstore outlets. Some authors sell
in-book ads and pay for all their printing costs this way.

You can include an order form and advertising for your other books at the back of your book. It's a great way to promote your titles indefinitely. Make sure you include the web address for your website, blog, and where your book can be purchased (Amazon!)

You can also sell advertising on your website. Ask companies or industries in the same general subject of your book if they would be willing to advertise on your website. We will cover web advertising more extensively later.

Advertising with Google AdWords

Google AdWords is exactly like AdSense except that YOU are the one advertising your product! If you have a niche product, you can use Google AdWords to direct traffic to your website and sell your books. I advertised with Google AdWords almost immediately after my first books went to print. I set up a "Starter Account" with Google, and set my monthly advertising budget at a maximum of $50 per month. You can set a daily and monthly maximum. Once you top out your advertising budget, your ad stops running.

After setting up your starter account, you need to create your ads. You create sample ads and choose keywords, which are words or phrases related to your book or business. You can get keyword ideas on the web. Just look up your competitors' websites.

Google ads work when someone enters your keywords into Google's search engines. Your ads then appear next to the search results. Your ad may not show up all the time—ads are all rotated by Google. Now you're advertising to an audience that's already interested in you. You are charged only when someone clicks on your ad.

How AdWords Works:

1. You create ads and choose keywords, which are words or phrases related to your business. Get keyword ideas by looking on the web for other ads.

2. Your ads appear on Google. When people search on Google using one of your keywords, your ad may appear next to the search results. Now you're advertising to an audience that's already interested in you.

3. You attract buyers. People can simply click your ad to purchase your book or learn more about you. If you don't have a website yet, Google will also help you create a website for free.[s]

People click on your ad to make a purchase or learn more about your books. You don't even need a webpage to join AdWords– Google will help you create one for free. No matter what your budget, you can display ads on Google and their advertising network. You pay only if people click your ads.[t] To sign up, go to *www.adwords.google.com*.

I personally believe that the majority of my sales come from my click ads on Google. When people search for study guides for the *IRS Enrolled Agent exam*, my ad pops up and takes potential customers to my website.

I pay a fee only when a user actually "clicks" on the ad. The reports on my website reflect that the majority of the traffic is generated from Google advertising.

I sell a niche product—books on taxation. And I found that the most cost-effective advertising for my books is Google AdWords. I check my traffic reports frequently. This is something you should learn to do. Using Microsoft's "reports" feature, I can see that the majority of my website's hits come from Google AdWords.

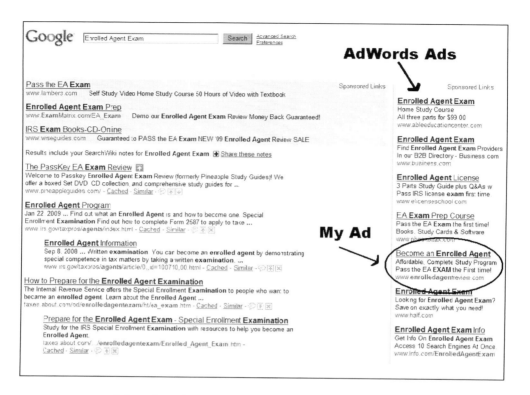

My advertisement shown on Google AdWords

Take some time to research Google's AdWords program for yourself. You can also try out different ads to see which ones generate the most traffic and sales on your website.

Create an Online Google Profile

Google is the Internet juggernaut. You can control how you appear in Google by creating a personal profile. You can use any e-mail address to form a Google account. If you already belong to a Google Group, then you already have an existing profile. You just need to set it up!

In less than a few days, your public profile will be bumped to the top of Google's search engines. When anyone searches for your book or your name on Google, your profile will pop up and all of your websites and your bio will be displayed. As I mentioned before, make sure you use your pen name, so your buyers can find you. It's free to create a Google profile, so create one right away, even if your book has not been published yet. Make sure you list all your websites in your Google profile. If you have a blog, website, or even just a MySpace page, list the URL. Your Google profile will look something like this:

My websites and blogs

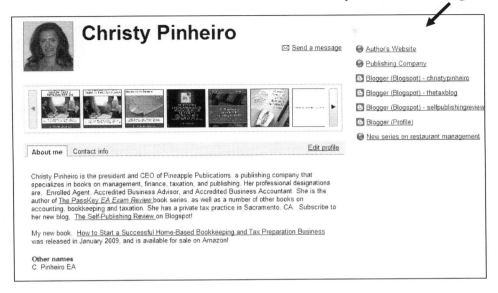

Christy's Public Profile on Google

You probably have a Google account already, if you belong to any Google NewsGroups, or if you have already signed up for Google AdWords or AdSense. If you want to create a completely different Google account using a new e-mail or password, you can do that too. You can post photos of yourself, or even better, post photos of all your books!

Facebook and Twitter Marketing

Facebook is an online social network; one of the most popular in the world. It's also a fantastic free marketing tool for authors and self-publishers. One of the best examples of Facebook that I've ever read was by author Perry Perkins. Perry is an award-winning travel writer, and the author of *Elk Hunter's Don't Cry*, a popular non-fiction book on outdoorsman activities.

He's granted us permission to reprint his experience.

Creating a Marketing Budget... With No Budget![ii]

In these economic times, the cost of printing, business cards, bookmarks, a few review copies, etc, etc...can quickly break a self-publisher's budget. Especially if, like me, you don't have a budget to start out with!

Most of what I've learned; I've learned the hard way, over a decade of self-publishing novels. I've picked up some tips and tricks along the way to support my writing when my bank account couldn't.

If you want a crash course on how easy it is to sell a self-published *non-fiction* book, publish *a novel* and spend a couple of years trying to market it yourself! (Make sure to budget for anti-depressants).

Starting at the beginning, I wanted 25-50 copies to send out to reviewers and business owners. My wholesale price for *Elk Hunters Don't Cry* is $3.00 a copy. This was based on a 70-book order.

I didn't spend a penny out of pocket. I created a ***"honeylist"*** of folks that were guaranteed to buy the book. These were friends, family, co-workers, etc. Then, I created several potential book covers (free with CreateSpace CoverCreator software and my own photos). I posted images of my favorite six covers to my blog. Then, I emailed everyone on my *honeylist*, and posted a link on my Facebook page, and Twitter page, announcing a cover contest. The cover that got the most votes would be chosen as the final cover.

Of the winning votes, I would draw a name. That winner would get a free, personally autographed copy of the book. I ended up with over 120 votes for the winning cover, and gave away two copies. I then added everyone who voted to my *honeylist*; expanding it from 50 contacts to over 300.

Once the cover was chosen, I wrote up a "pre-order" promotional email, with an embedded PayPal link (including shipping charges), allowing everyone on my *honeylist* to order an autographed copy of the book in advance. I included a link in the promotional e-mail to a webpage that had the cover, a synopsis, a sample story, a PayPal link (again) as well as a printable order form. I *still* didn't even have a proof copy of my book. Total out-of-pocket was *zero*.

Within two weeks, I had 41 **pre-paid orders**. After a celebratory dinner at Taco Bell with my wife, that left me with $600! This covered the cost of the ProPlan upgrade ($39) a new box of VistaPrint business cards, ($10), 70 books ($210.00), a handful of Starbucks gift-cards (to give away in future promotions) and plenty left over for shipping and materials, and maybe some professional bookmarks with the cover and eStore address.

It also left me with 25 copies of the book to send to reviewers. All of this, with nothing out-of-pocket. I've had several more orders since then, and plan to see a goodly number when my pre-order customers start showing their copies around (oh, and a sent out a detailed review request, printed and folded into each book, as well.)

The next batch of books I order will go with me to the Northwest Sportsman's Expo, where I plan to spend a VERY long day schmoozing store owners and magazine editors. Each book will have a flyer inside that explains how to order books directly from me at 30% off the cover-price. The flyer will also have the Amazon and eStore links.

I'm still hitting all my social networks, answering (non-book related) questions, engaging in conversation, laughing at jokes, and making sure that the sweet little eStore link always appears under my name.

Perry P. Perkins is the author of Elk Hunters Don't Cry. Perry has written for numerous magazines and anthologies. His inspirational stories have been included in twelve Chicken Soup for The Soul anthologies.

Affiliate Marketing for Big Bucks

Affiliate marketing is the practice of using one website to drive traffic to another. You can make your website a hub for affiliate marketing. Affiliate marketing works a little differently from pay-per-click advertising like Google's AdWords. There are a lot opportunities to make money through affiliate marketing. Every time you drive another customer to your website, there's a chance you will generate affiliate revenues, AdWords revenues, and revenues from the final sale of your book. All of these ads work together to promote your books, your website, and your Amazon listings.

There are a lot of great affiliate marketing programs out there.

Amazon's Affiliate Program

Amazon Associates was one of the first online affiliate marketing programs. When website owners and bloggers create links and customers click through those links and buy products from Amazon, they earn referral fees. It's free to join and easy to use.

Join Amazon's affiliate program right away. It's a great way to start promoting your Amazon listings directly on your website. When you sign up to be an Amazon affiliate, you are able to produce a "widget" for your book. A widget is an advertising tool that you can use on your website to promote your book. Once you publish your book with CreateSpace and the listing appears on Amazon, you just go to the Amazon Associates website and click on the link that says "Product Links." This will allow you to create a little widget that promotes only your book.

It will ask for your ISBN, you enter that, and Amazon Associates will create the HTML code for you to post on your website. Once you post the code, you will see an advertisement appear that promotes your book. When surfers visit your website and click on the link, you will earn up to 8.5 percent if they complete a purchase on Amazon.

You can make even more when you advertise other Amazon products, such as Amazon's Kindle and AmazonMP3. You can experiment with different links on your website and your blog in order to see which ads generate the most revenue for you. Amazon Associates also provides reports so you can see which ads generate the most revenue. You can adjust your website to feature only the ads that drive referrals and profits. It's really that simple!

Affiliate marketing is even more profitable than pay-per-click ads because you can earn money multiple ways. You earn referral fees when a buyer clicks on your website and completes a purchase. Then you also earn book royalties if the book purchased is yours.

Chapter 11: Interviews and Book Promotion Techniques

"I've never met an author that was sorry he or she wrote their book . . . they are only sorry they did not write it sooner."

—**Sam Horn**, Author and Speaker

Interview with Jan Axelson

Lakeview Research
www.lvr.com

Jan Axelson is the author of multiple technical books, and the founder of Lakeview Research, a small independent press. Most of her books relate to computers. She has been self-publishing successfully since 1994. Jan's books are the example of a perfected niche product. She promotes her books exclusively online.

So, how did you get started in the world of self-publishing?

Jan: Previously, I published with a large traditional publisher, and I did the self-published book as an experiment, to compare my experiences. I never looked back.

This seems to be a common theme with self-published authors. Many publish their book using a traditional publisher, and either had a bad experience, or just decided that they wanted more freedom. When you published with the traditional publisher, did you have a bad experience?

Jan: Well, the book [with the traditional publisher] did fine. It only recently went out of print. But the time lag is a real problem… it takes so much longer for a traditional publisher to get a book out.

That's probably changed a bit for some books now, but there's also the control issue. How much control do you want to have over your book? There's the money issue too. You earn more doing it yourself. You have more work, but the payback is better.

You say that it takes longer to publish a book with a traditional publisher. Obviously your books are about technology, which seems to change all the time. Your books have to be timely.

Jan: Yes. I just did the fourth edition of my USB book, *USB Complete: the Developer's Guide*. I update a title every few years if changes in technology or software warrant it. My most recent update was after four years. I have another book, *Serial Port Complete*, which is in its second edition. It's a major project to do a book update, so I don't update the books every year.

How do you keep yourself up-to-date in your field?

Jan: Well, a lot of the information is online, and I attend trade shows. I do a lot of my own research and experiments. I write programming and test out the products. I put the information together, and I write about the experience. It's a combination of research and experimenting.

Do you fulfill your own orders?

Jan: No, since 1996, I've had trade distribution. For my first book, I did it all myself, and I never enjoyed it. I didn't have an alternative when I was starting, but as soon as I was able to get trade distribution, I jumped on it. I have no interest in fulfilling orders!

Once you reach a certain level of success, you either have to hire someone to do part of the work for you, or do it with a distributor. There just aren't enough hours in the day to do it all.

The first year that you started, how did you get your books printed? Did you use POD or a vanity publisher?

Jan: This was at the very beginning when the DocuTech printers came out (these were the original printers that they used for Print-On-Demand). We had a local printer that purchased one, so I used them. I made a PDF of my book, and they would print up to 200 copies at a time for me. It was really nice because it only took a week. So I could put an order in and deliver the books really quickly.

So I found a local printer that essentially had POD capability. There were no Print-On-Demand publishers back in 1994. This worked fine for me at the beginning.

How about marketing?

Jan: Well, when I started, I took out magazine ads. But I was also working freelance for some magazines, and I was able to write some articles that would promote the books. So I had some publicity there.

I got into a few catalogs that were selling for me. At that point, it was successful enough that I decided that I would continue.

Do you continue to write freelance articles for trade magazines?

Jan: A little bit. Mainly I do magazine articles as a way to gain publicity for my books. I used to do a little technical writing on the side, but I've quit doing that. I have enough to do with the books.

When you market your books, do you do it exclusively online, or do you go to trade shows, etc?

Jan: No, it's all online. I did go to a trade show last year, but it was more of an educational event, rather than a promotional one. I also cross-promote different titles simply by mentioning them in my books, since the material is interrelated. Amazon typically pairs my books together.

You have six books on your website that are currently in publication. Is that correct?

Jan: Yes. Lakeview Research has six titles in print. The seventh one, *Making Printed Circuit Boards*, is from McGraw Hill and is either out of print or close to it.

Do you have employees that help you run the business?

Jan: Well, not exactly. I hire out the index and cover design. I obviously don't do the printing, but it's the distributor that takes the big load off of me. It's just me, but I have a distributor that does all the grunt work. The distributor does all the sales, the billing, the storage; they handle foreign rights for me. So I'm happy to give them a percentage. They take care of all of it.

So you have foreign rights to your book too. How does that work?

Jan: I sell the rights to the books and the translation is handled by someone else. It's similar to other traditional publishing contracts. Typically I receive an advance and when the advance is earned out, the contract pays royalties.

The bulk of your revenues still comes from self-publishing, though.

Jan: Yes. I have some revenues from the website. I have advertising on the website that generates revenue. I have Google ads, and I have a few private advertisers that pay me individually to place an advertisement on my website.

Do you feel that the day-to-day financial and business tasks are difficult to manage?

Jan: No, I actually enjoy it. I only spend a few hours a month doing financial and bookkeeping tasks, and everything else is taken care of by the distributor. Having a website makes things easier. I spend another few hours a week working on the website and doing other promotional tasks. The rest of my time is spent doing research and writing.

Self-publishing isn't easy. It isn't just about selling. It's not rocket science, but it takes effort and skill and hard work. It takes dedication to be successful.

Do you have anything else that you'd like to add?

Jan: Well, I'd say that self-publishing works really well for some of us, and not for others. You have to enjoy running a business. It's a mindset. A lot of writers don't want to run a business. You have to have a tolerance for managing your business, beyond writing the books. If you do, then it can work out really well.

Interview with Nick Russell

As the founder of the *Gypsy Journal*, Nick Russell does most of his marketing face-to-face. In this interview, he discusses how he's developed his successful business strategies:

You have an extensive background in the newspaper industry.

Nick: Yes, I have twenty-five years of experience in the newspaper and publishing industry. I started out publishing local newspapers. I like the *Gypsy Journal* newspaper because I don't have to cover politics, school board meetings, and boring stuff like that. Now I just write about fun stuff.

On your website, you mention that you were extremely nervous the first time you spoke in front of a group. How did you get over stage fright?

Nick: Before I gave my first speech, I threw up three times. It was very hard for me the first time. But now, I love it. I was taking myself too seriously, not wanting to make a mistake. A friend of mine who's an accomplished speaker told me, "The [audience] is dumb. They think that you're the expert. No matter what you say, they're going to listen to you."

Unlike other authors, you do the majority of your marketing face-to-face. Have you always done that?

Nick: Yes, from the very beginning. For our book, ***Meandering Down the Highway***, that was an important part of our marketing. We made it a point to go to RV events and talk to our customers one-on-one. We give them a complimentary copy of the *Gypsy Journal* and let them read it. From day one, we have always done the majority of our marketing face-to-face.

Do you use your seminars to generate back-of-the-room sales?

Nick: I don't push people—I actually try to downplay it. I talk to the audience about the subject at hand, like highway history or travel tips. I let them know that the books are available. If we have a vendor booth, I'll mention that.

I'm selling myself. I'm just telling stories. Hopefully, the audience will like them. I want to impart the knowledge—that's the main reason why I agree to do speaking engagements. I don't make sales goals for myself, though. I don't say, "I have to sell fifty books during this seminar." I go there to talk to people and give them information that they can use. I feel that if they've learned something, I've done my job. It does sell a lot of books for us, though!

Usually, my wife Terry is at our booth while I am speaking. After the seminar, people usually stick around to talk to me, with specific questions or whatever. By the time I get to our booth, Terry is usually swamped with people trying to buy books.

So the seminars ARE a marketing tactic!

Nick: Yes, of course. Obviously this is how we make our living, but I enjoy teaching and talking to groups so much that I don't let the pressure of sales get to me. The very first RV show we went to, we attended a seminar with two well-known authors. The seminar was all high pressure sales: "Buy our book, buy our book!"

It turned off everyone in the audience. Afterwards, there was a man who approached the authors. He was a fan. He had several of the author's books already, and he asked for an autograph. The author said, "We have new copies for sale in the back of the room; if you want me to sign them, you'll have to purchase a new book."

He [the fan] was so upset that he threw the books in the trash and walked out—right in front of everyone.

That's horrible!

Nick: Yeah, I never wanted to come across that way. I want to share with my readers. "Hey, I'm here to share with you, and the books are available, but let's not worry about that right now."

For most authors, marketing doesn't come naturally. Your business model is really customer-friendly, and that's part of your success. That attitude must be part of your success.

Nick: Yes, I believe so. Buyers come up to us and tell us that they appreciate that we are "down to earth." We just try to be ourselves and buyers like that.

You are a firm believer that book reviews sell books. But it seems that most self-published authors haven't really learned that lesson.

Nick: You have to spend money on reviews. I mean, you don't purchase the actual review, but you must be willing to send out free review copies to reviewers. That's your advertising. You have to give reviewers copies of your book. It's just the cost of doing business. If you had a storefront, you'd have to pay for a sign.

When you self-publish, you **have to** give away free review copies. It's the cheapest advertising you can buy.

Do you feel like the re-sale of review copies is an issue?

Nick: No, I really haven't encountered a problem. In the newspaper business, we give away enormous numbers of free review copies. In my opinion, when I send someone a review copy, they can do whatever they want with the book. As long as I get a review, I'm happy.

There are lots of people out there that want to do what we're doing. But you have to be able to write **and** market your work. You can't do just one thing. It doesn't matter how many great books you write—if people don't know they're out there, you aren't going to succeed. Your books will just sit in a box someplace. We have a website, we have a blog, we have an e-store, and we also aggressively market our books in person.

The publishing market is changing rapidly. Since you are on the road all the time, how do you manage your products? Do you carry inventory?

Nick: We carry very little inventory because we use Lightning Source. They are our Print-On-Demand publisher. I call them when I need to order copies, and they send them to any address that I want. Because we travel in a motor home, we can't carry large amounts of inventory.

A lot of our success is because we sell very little inventory through traditional outlets. Our books are available on Amazon, but I don't mess with any bookstores myself. I don't want to. I find that my time is much better spent face-to-face with customers. Our product is a recreational product. For what we do, "face-to-face" is the best way to market our products.

So, your profit margins are higher when you sell books at your rallies and speaking events.

Nick: Yes, much higher. I'd rather sell fewer copies, but at a higher profit margin and develop relationships with my readers.

Interview with Dan Poynter

By Misti Sandefur

Dan Poynter
Case Study of Success

Have you heard of Dan Poynter? No? Well, he's not as famous as Stephen King or J.K. Rowling, but he's still a bestselling author and a very wealthy man. And he got rich publishing books about a subject that he loves, namely parachutes and hang gliding.

Dan Poynter was a self-published success story from the very beginning. Dan's first book was a "500-page technical treatise on parachutes." He realized quickly that he couldn't get a publisher to even look at it, so he published it himself. To date, he has published over 120 books, including spin-offs such as audiotapes, videotapes, magazine excerpts, foreign language editions, and more.

Dan has sold millions of his books, including several bestsellers, for tens of millions of dollars in sales. Many of his individual books sell at the rate of 10-20,000 copies per year, every year.[v] Don't you want a taste of the same success?

Dan Poynter began self-publishing when he started writing books on subjects (parachutes and hang gliding) he knew publishers wouldn't be interested in. Because he knew publishers wouldn't take an interest in the genres he chose, he took it upon himself to find a printer and self-publish his own books. Not only did he take on the responsibility of publishing on his own, but Poynter also took on the marketing role.

Later, when Poynter's books were ready to sell, he proved to the whole world that self-publishing your own book could bring you success. *Hang Gliding*, Poynter's second self-published book, became a bestseller when it sold more than 130,000 copies! This man is the one you want to learn from if you're considering the self-publishing route.

Now, don't think you can just write a book, find a printer, and then—voila!—you're successful. Self-publishing isn't that easy—there's a lot of toil, time, and effort involved. However, don't let the process scare you away. If you have a book that has an audience, but you are certain that traditional publishers won't look at it, then give self-publishing a shot. Poynter's book, *The Self-Publishing Manual: How to Write, Print and Sell Your Own Book*, will give you valuable information that you need to be successful.

At what age did you discover you were born to write?

Dan: I am not sure I have discovered that yet. We are all in the information business. We deliver our expertise in several ways: writing, speaking, etc., and writing is just one of the delivery methods.

Congratulations on your great self-publishing success! Can you share some of the marketing techniques you used to become successful?

Dan: Before you start writing, make sure there is a market for your proposed book and that you can reach it. Identify and be able to locate people interested in your subject. Write what you love and sell to your friends.

I began with books on parachutes and skydiving. I am a skydiver and was a parachute designer, and I know how to reach my market through parachute stores, skydiving centers, skydiving clubs, parachute catalogs, the International Parachute Symposium, and so on.

How do you find ideas for your books?

Dan: Write what you love. Turn your passion center into your profit center. Turn your avocation into your vocation.

Can you share any advice with other writers/authors on how they too can make their books a success?

Dan: Promotion is up to you. Publishers do not promote books. Your promotion plan is more important than your writing plan. Without promotion, no one will know you have written. The first three things that should be done:
>   1. Send out review copies.
>   2. Send articles to magazines in your field.
>   3. Send e-mail announcements to everyone in your own e-mail address book.

Did you try the traditional publishing route before you chose to self-publish?

Dan: My first book was a 500-page technical treatise on parachutes. Realizing no publisher would buy it—or even understand it—I published myself. Since then I've sold manuscripts to publishers and I've published other authors. I have a wide range of experience.

What were some of the mistakes you made with your first self-published book, and what did you learn from those mistakes?

Dan: Not knowing that magazines and newsletters would review your book for free! I did not know you could send review copies to publications. If you would like a list of more than ninety categories of magazines that you can send your book to review, see:
http://parapublishing.com/sites/para/resources/maillist.cfm.

In *The Self-Publishing Manual: How to Write, Print and Sell Your Own Book,* you discuss bookstore chains, and you said, "The best way to approach larger bookstore chains is to have a distributor's sales rep visit," but what if the author makes the visit? Can you give other authors a few tips on how they can get their book onto the shelves of the larger bookstore chains (Barnes & Noble, Borders, etc.) if they decided to approach the bookstores on their own?

Dan: Individual author-publishers can call the chains and try to get an appointment, but distributors have an existing relationship with them. But I can call my distributor's rep and the fix will be made overnight. Do not underestimate the value of a distributor.

If you still want to know more about book writing, publishing, and promoting, and get Poynter's free information kits, visit his website, www.ParaPublishing.comᵂ

Your Self-Publishing Journey

The Internet has changed the publishing landscape forever. The web makes it possible for you to self-publish, self-promote, and build your own writing business from the comfort of a home office.

With today's computerized Print-On-Demand (POD) technology, anybody with a home computer and a couple of relatively inexpensive programs can write a book, format it at home, design a cover, and publish a book for under $500. Then you can market your own book and keep all of the profits, rather than sharing with agents and publishers. Because you don't have the high up-front costs, the risk of bringing out a new book is negligible.

Print-On-Demand books cost more per single copy than printing with traditional methods, but the extra cost is offset by not having to spend a huge amount of money up front, not having to store thousands of books until sold, and the speed with which you can publish a new book. Once you are established with a POD printer, the turnaround time for submitting a manuscript to having a proof in hand can be less than a week.

And once the proof is approved, you can order as many copies as you wish, and have them printed and shipped within a week. This allows you to do your own marketing with review copies, sales from your website, and other sales. Print-On-Demand publishing cuts out the middleman and lets you deal directly with the retailer. The biggest book retailer is Amazon.

Amazon is America's largest online marketplace, and self-publishing with CreateSpace will get your book listed fast!

I wish you great success in all of your publishing endeavors. Now get out there and write!

Essential Reading

I've read all these books and recommend them personally. All of them are well-written, easy to read, and will help you make money as a self-published author.

1. Aaron Shepard. *Aiming at Amazon.* In my opinion, this is the best book currently on the market for promoting your book exclusively on Amazon.

2. Aaron Shepard. *Perfect Pages.* You must buy this book if you want to format your book yourself in Microsoft Word. This book covers book formatting in Word 97-2003 for Windows and Word 2004 for the Mac.

3. Morris Rosenthal. *Print-on-Demand Book Publishing.* Rosenthal's book is a great resource for a beginner. He goes over the basics of the publishing industry and the information is concise and well-delivered. The Kindle edition of this book is less than $2.

4. Dan Poynter. *The Self Publishing Manual.* This is one of the great "Bibles" of the self-publishing industry. Poynter still uses more traditional methods (he carries inventory and does most of his own order fulfillment). But the book is still a "must have" for any beginner. This is the first book on self-publishing that I ever read. It made me believe that I could do it.

5. Peter Bowerman. *The Well-Fed Self-Publisher.* Bowerman's book is funny, informative, and contains lots of great information that will teach you how to self-publish profitably. Although Bowerman isn't a fan of POD, he is a marketing genius. His book is full of resources on how to market your book to different audiences. He'll tell you what a terrible press release looks like and how to avoid getting stuck with a garage full of useless inventory.

6. Patricia Fry. *The Right Way to Write, Publish and Sell Your Book.* This is an excellent book for any writer, even those who are looking to publish traditionally. But Fry's best pointers are about how to promote your book regionally. This is a must-have if you are trying to promote your book to a specific region or local market.

Important Resources for Self-Publishing

www.absolutewrite.com
Absolutewrite is one of the best and most basic resources for writers. It's an online magazine for beginning writers and professional writers. It covers fiction, nonfiction, screenwriting, freelance writing, novels, playwriting, and other genres.

www.asja.org
The American Society of Journalists and Authors is the largest national organization for freelance nonfiction authors.

www.BookMarket.com
The Book Market is a great website that offers free information on book marketing. There's a lot to look through here, and some of it is shameless advertising, but the website is still a great resource.

www.cwfi-online.org
The Christian Writers Fellowship International is a Christian-based writing support organization. Yearly membership dues are $45.

www.matilijapress.com
Patricia Fry is a successful self-published writer and her website and blog are a goldmine of free information for authors looking to self-publish. She is also a successful editor and offers freelance writing and promotion services. Her blog is one of the best free resources on the web for self-published authors.

www.marinbookworksblog.com
For interior book design and consulting, I recommend **Marin Bookworks.** An experienced publisher, book designer and self-published author, Joel Friedlander is the founder of Marin Bookworks, a publisher-services company in CA, the author of Body Types, The Enneagram of Essence Types, and blogs about issues of interest to new and experienced publishers at *www.theBookDesigner.com.* He's also a great guy.

www.newselfpublishing.com
This is Aaron Shepard's publishing page. Make sure you visit his website if you are even THINKING about publishing with LightningSource.

www.pma-online.org
The Independent Book Publishers Association (formerly PMA) is an organization open to self-published authors and independents. There's a lot of information about book marketing on this website.

www.publishersmarketplace.com
Publishers Marketplace provides membership information for publishing professionals and provides web pages for writers and agents to promote themselves.

www.publishing4profit.com
This is Nick Russell's informational website for self-published authors. There's a lot of great information here.

www.selfpublishingresources.com
This is Marilyn and Tom Ross's website. They are the authors of various popular books on self-publishing, including *The Complete Guide to Self-Publishing*. Go to the "free resources" tab and check out the good information there.

www.sfwa.org/beware
Writer Beware is the public face of the Science Fiction and Fantasy Writers of America's Committee on Writing Scams.

www.spannet.org
The Small Publisher's Association of North America (SPAN) is a non-profit organization for small publishers. There's great information for start-ups. SPAN gives partner discounts when you join if you already belong to a partner organization (like SPAWN).

www.Spawn.org.
The Small Publishers, Artists, and Writers Network provides opportunities for everyone involved in publishing. The site offers information on writing and publishing. It also offers links to research sources, publishers, printers, and the media.

www.writerswrite.com
This is a great resource on writing and publishing, with thousands of pages dedicated to writing, publishing, and promotion.

Additional Contributors

1. **Michael Pollick.** *Should a Writer Use a Pen Name?* Michael is a freelance writer and frequent contributor to *www.wiseGEEK.com*, a division of Conjecture Corporation.

2. **Carol Leonard.** *Why I Chose to Self-Publish.* Carol is a successful midwife and self-published author.

3. **Misti Sandefur.** *Interview with Dan Poynter.* Misty is a self-published Christian author. Her website is *www.mistisandefur.com*.

4. **Perry Perkins,** *Creating a Marketing Budget… With No Budget!* Perry is the award-winning author of *Elk Hunters Don't Cry*.

Index

Aaron Shepard. *See* Shepard, Aaron
Absolute Write, 54, 170
Adobe Acrobat, 95
Adobe InDesign, 94
Adobe Reader, 96
AdSense, 146
Advertising
    on Craigslist, 90
    website, 148
    with Adwords, 148
    within a book, 148
AdWords, 148
Affiliate marketing, 153
Agents, 25
Aiming at Amazon, 94
Amazon, 61, 127
    author's profile, 111
    BookSurge, 29
    CreateSpace, 27
    Look Inside, 41, 65
    testimonials, 128
American Society of Journalists and Authors, 170
ASJA, 170
Atlanta Nights, 21
Author Central, 112
Author mill, 21
Author's photo, 99
Author's profiles, 111
Aweber, 141
Axelson, Jan, 24, 157
B2B sales, 24
Back-up devices, 56
Beaumont, Dale, 120
Bibliography, 65
Biographies, 40
Blog, 145
Blurb, 31
Book formatting, 94
Book reviews, 127, 132
Book series, 117
Book signings, 120
Bookkeeping, 50
Bookland EAN, 85
BookMarket, 170
Books in Print. *See* BowkerLink
BookSurge, 29
Bowker, 75, 83
BowkerLink, 86
Budget, 65
Business connections, 121

Business entity, 75
Business expenses, 49
Business income, 49
Business records, 52
Business-to-business sales, 24
Cell phone, 53
Christian Writers Fellowship International, 170
Comb binding, 70
Commercial publishers, 19
Company name, 137
Competition, 41
Compounding profits, 117
Conventions, 144
Copy editor, 22, 89, 90
Copyrights, 83
Corporation, 75
Cover
    graphics, 63
    photography, 63
    typos, 100
CoverCreator, 63
CPA, 51, 66
Craigslist, 90
CreateSpace, 70
    history of, 27
    new account, 91
    royalties, 71
Credit cards, 50
Direct mail, 127
DocuTech printers, 158
Domain name, 137
Dreamstime, 100
EAN Bar Code, 85
eBook Architects, 97
Editor, 62
EIN, 76
E-mail address, 140
E-mail list, 66
E-mail newsletter, 140
Employee records, 51
Employer identification number, 76
Enrolled Agent, 51, 66
Entity classification, 75
Expanded Distribution Channel, 28
Facebook, 151
Fax line, 53
Fiction, 40, 89
Fictitious business name, 48
Fonts, 98
Footnotes, 65
Formatting, 94, 104

Fraud, 51
Fry, Patricia, 61
General partner, 77
Genre, 39, 46
GettyImages, 100
Goals, 42
Google
    AdSense, 146
    AdWords, 148
Grammar errors, 105
Gullery, Jonathan, 34
Gypsy Journal, 24, 41, 121, 144, 145
Home office, 55
Home Office Deduction, 80
Hook, 101
Hosting companies, 137
HTML editing, 138
Imprints, 47, 93
Income, 56
Indexing, 64
Ingram, 32
International Standard Book Number, 46
Internet, 168, *See* websites
Inventory, 61
IRS, 51
ISBN, 75, 83, 84
Istockphoto, 100
Keywords, 62, 149
Kindle, 154
Kindle formatting, 97
Lady's Hands, Lion's Heart, 33
Lakeview Research, 24, 157
Layout, 63
Leonard, Carol, 33
Liability insurance, 76
Lightning Source, 31
Limited Liability Company, 77
List price, 102
LLC, 77
Look Inside, 41, 65
Lulu, 29
Magazine ads, 158
Marin Bookworks, 170
Marketing
    AdWords, 148
    anchor, 117
    blogging, 145
    book fairs, 120
    book signings, 120
    direct mail, 127
    direct sales, 61
    e-mail marketing, 141
    e-mail signature, 142
    existing customers, 119
    fiction, 40
    locally, 23
    niche, 22
    pen names, 44

press releases, 66
    regional, 23
    secondary audience, 41
    special reports, 120
Marketing potential, 39
Matilija Press, 170
Meandering Down The Highway, 144
Memberships, 53
Microsoft Live Small Business, 138
Microsoft Word, 64
Midwest Book Review, 131
Mileage, 52
Mulvany, Nancy, 64
myidentifiers, 84
Networking, 53
Newsletter, 119, 140
Niche market, 22, 117
Nick Russell. *See* Russell, Nick
nom de plume. *See* Pen Name
Nonfiction, 15, 39, 40
Operating expenses, 80
Order fulfillment, 61
Organizations, 54
Owner draw, 50
Page counts, 71
Partnership, 77
PayPal, 138, 152
Pay-Per-Click, 153
PDF converter, 95
Pen name, 43
    anonymity, 45
    ethnic, 44
Perfect Pages, 94
Perkins, Perry, 151
Permission form, 131
Phone, 53
Photo-books, 29
POD. *See* print-on-demand
Poynter, Dan, 61, 165
Press releases, 66
Pricing, 102
Primo PDF, 96
Print advertising, 127
Print-On-Demand, 19, 20
    Blurb, 31
Product Links, 153
Professional layout, 63
Professional organizations, 53
Profile, 111
Profits, 117, 142
Promotion
    traditional publishers, 26
Proof, 105, 106
Proofreading, 62
ProPlan, 29, 152
Pseudonym. *See* Pen Name
Public profile, 111
Publicity. *See* Marketing

PublishAmerica, 21
Publishers Marketplace, 171
Publishing company, 84
Publishing4Profit, 171
QuarkXPress, 94
Quoted sources, 65
Recordkeeping, 51
Records, 52
Regional subjects, 23
Re-seller's permit, 24
Retail margin, 102
Revenue, 56, 119, *See* also Royalties
Royalties, 71
Russell, Nick, 120, 121, 144, 171, 177
RV trade shows, 121
Sales tax, 24
Sans Serif font, 98
Scams, 19
    review copies, 128
    vanity publishers, 19
Scanned records, 52
Search engines, 138
Search Inside this Book, 65
Secondary audience, 41
Self-Publishing, 20, 27, 46, 61, 75, 81
Seller's permit, 24
Seminars, 120
Series, 117
Serif font, 97
Share publishers, 19
Shepard, Aaron, 32, 86, 94, 111, 169
Social networking, 140
Software, 57
Sole-proprietorship, 76
SPAN, 171
Spawn, 54, 64, 171
Special Reports, 120
Stage name, 43
Standard Book Numbering, 46

Stock photography, 63
Student discounts, 57
Submission requirements, 104
Subsidy publishers, 19
Table of contents, 64
Target market, 41, 62, 117
Tax deductions, 52
Taxes, 50
Telephone number, 53
Testimonials, 128, 138
Title
    avoiding duplicates, 92
    choosing a title, 62
    set up on CreateSpace, 92
Toastmasters, 120
Tracfone, 53
Trademarks, 82
Traditional publishers, 35
Trim size, 71, 94
Twitter, 152
Typefaces, 63
Unagented authors, 25
Vanity publisher, 21
VOIP line, 53
Web hosting, 137
Webinars, 120
Website, 137, 148
    blog, 145
    free from Microsoft, 138
    free from Weebly, 139
    testimonials, 131
Weebly, 139
Wholesale pricing, 23
Widget, 153
Writer Beware, 171
Writer's block, 42
Writer's Market, 53
Yearbooks, 29

About the Authors

About Christy Pinheiro, EA ABA

Christy Pinheiro is an Enrolled Agent, Accredited Business Advisor®, and financial writer. She is the author of thirteen books. Her finance and tax articles have been nationally published online and in various periodicals. She is a member of the National Association of Tax Professionals.

Among Christy's books is a complete study guide series for the IRS Enrolled Agent Exam. Her personal website is *www.ChristyPinheiro.com*.

Her publishing company is PassKey Publications at *www.PassKeyPublications.com*. See her blog, The Publishing Maven, at *www.selfpublishingreview.blogspot.com*

About Nick Russell

Nick is a popular and dynamic speaker, and has presented seminars at campgrounds, RV rallies, and special events across the country. He is the founder of the popular **Gypsy Journal** newspaper and the author of **Meandering Down the Highway**.

You can reach Nick through his website, *www.gypsyjournal.net*, or by mail at: Nick Russell, *Gypsy Journal* RV Travel Newspaper, 1400 Colorado Street #C-16, Boulder City, Nevada 89005

Endnotes

[a] Science Fiction and Fantasy Writers of America. Writer Beware! Warnings About Literary Fraud and Other Schemes, Scams, and Pitfalls That Target Writers.

[b] Sci Fi Wire. SF Authors Sting Publisher. www.scifi.com.

[c] Nick Russell. The Truth About the Publishing Business. Used with permission.

[d] Carol Leonard has just self-published the bestseller, *Lady's Hands, Lion's Heart: A Midwife's Saga* (Bad Beaver Publishing, 2008). **www.badbeaverpublishing.com**

[e] The Talk of the Book World Still Can't Sell. St. John, Warren. The New York Times.

[f] Michael Pollick, "Should a Writer Use a Pen Name?" Used with permission.

[g] An Enrolled Agent (EA) is a federally-authorized tax practitioner who has technical expertise in the field of taxation. That's what I am!

[h] CreateSpace help index. Book Industry Terms.

[i] CreateSpace. Content License Royalties.

[j] Enrolled Agents, also called "EAs," (that's what I am) are federally licensed tax practitioners.

[k] www.IRS.gov. IRS enforcement data.

[l] Nick Russell. *Publishing 4 Profit*. Used with permission.

[m] I did not receive any compensation for recommending my attorney in this book. I just thought their service was great, and that I would spread the word.

[n] U.S. Copyright Office. Copyright in general. www.copyright.gov/help

[o] Dan Poynter. Para Publishing. About Dan Poynter.

[p] Nick Russell, The Right Niche Can Make You Rich! Used with permission.

[q] Nick Russell. Publishing 4 Profit. Used with Permission.

[r] Darren Rowse. ProBlogger Survey. www.ProBlogger.com. *A Reality Check about Blogging for Money*.

[s] How AdWords Works. Google AdWords information. www.adwords.google.com

[t] Google AdWords information. www.adwords.google.com

[u] Perry Perkins. *Creating a Marketing Budget… With No Budget!* Used with permission.

[v] Dan Poynter, Para Publishing. www.parapublishing.com

[w] Misti Sandefur. Interview with Dan Poynter. *www.mistisandefur.com*

38184987R00101

Made in the USA
Middletown, DE
14 December 2016